Fish pies and
French fries,
vegetables,
meat and
something
sweet…

Visit our How To website at www.howto.co.uk

At **www.howto.co.uk** you can engage in conversation with our authors – all of whom have 'been there and done that' in their specialist fields. You can get access to special offers and additional content but most importantly you will be able to engage with, and become a part of, a wide and growing community of people just like yourself.

At **www.howto.co.uk** you'll be able to talk and share tips with people who have similar interests and are facing similar challenges in their lives. People who, just like you, have the desire to change their lives for the better – be it through moving to a new country, starting a new business, growing their own vegetables, or writing a novel.

At **www.howto.co.uk** you'll find the support and encouragement you need to help make your aspirations a reality.

You can go direct to **www.fish-pies-and-french-fries.co.uk** which is part of the main How To site.

How To Books strives to present authentic, inspiring, practical information in their books. Now, when you buy a title from **How To Books**, you get even more than just words on a page.

howtobooks

Please send for a free copy of the latest catalogue:
How To Books
Spring Hill House, Spring Hill Road,
Begbroke, Oxford OX5 1RX, United Kingdom
www.howtobooks.co.uk

Fish pies and French fries, vegetables, meat and something

sweet…affordable, everyday food and family-friendly recipes MADE EASY

(for busy people with a lot on their plate)

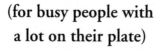

More simple, wholesome and nutritious recipes from the author of *How to feed your whole family…*

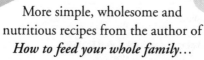

GILL HOLCOMBE

Spring Hill

Published by Spring Hill

Spring Hill is an imprint of
How To Books Ltd
Spring Hill House, Spring Hill Road
Begbroke, Oxford OX5 1RX, United Kingdom.
Tel: (01865) 375794 Fax: (01865) 379162
info@howtobooks.co.uk
www.howtobooks.co.uk

British Library Cataloguing in Publication Data.
A catalogue record for this book is available
from the British Library.

ISBN: 978 1 905862 33 7

Cover design by Baseline Arts Ltd
Produced for Spring Hill Books by Deer Park Productions, Tavistock
Typeset by Baseline Arts Ltd
Printed and bound in Great Britain by Bell & Bain Ltd, Glasgow

Mixed Sources

Product group from well-managed
forests and other controlled sources
www.fsc.org Cert no. TT-COC-002769
© 1996 Forest Stewardship Council

FSC

To Carole, with love and gratitude

"To make your food interesting, serve what you really like the way you really like it."

Lee Bailey

Acknowledgements

A very big thank you to Carole Moore, Claire Hack, Debbie Finlay, Pam Sinyor, Ann Kent, Gill Danis and my mum for passing on tips and recipe ideas; to Andrea Bovee and Janet Snowman for work behind the scenes; also Vicki McIvor at Take Three Management; everyone at Spring Hill and Deer Park Productions; Jennifer Gregory; and finally, my three children, Oliver, Billy and Eleanor, even though one of them went vegetarian and the other two are hardly ever at home.

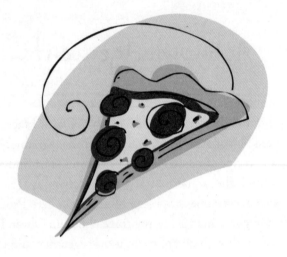

"Give me neither poverty nor riches; feed me with food convenient for me."

Proverbs

Contents

4. For starters, mains and just desserts / 209

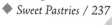

5. Something sweet / 257

PIZZA

6. A lot on your plate / 287

MENUS

WHAT REVIEWERS HAVE SAID ABOUT GILL HOLCOMBE'S FIRST BOOK

How to feed your whole family a healthy, balanced diet, with very little money and hardly any time, even if you have a tiny kitchen, only three saucepans (one with an ill-fitting lid) and no fancy gadgets – unless you count the garlic crusher ...

'Publishing phenomenon of the year!' *Mail on Sunday*

'One of the publishing sensations of 2009. The robust guide with handy tips and recipes for dishes such as chilli con carne and chicken nuggets has climbed into the bestseller lists and been reprinted four times in the past 12 months.' *The Independent*

'No-nonsense: Gill's low-cost approach to cookery is winning her an army of fans, especially during the recession.' *Daily Mail*

'Packed with labour and money-saving tips, and it's a great buy for any busy mother. You can make a nutritious meal ... in the time it takes to dial up and wait for a pizza.' *BBC Good Food Magazine*

'A brilliant little volume in which the hearty, honest, family friendly recipes are delicious.' *The Sunday Times, Style Magazine. Reviewer India Knight, author of The Thrift Book*

'Reveals the secrets of cooking on a budget.' *Daily Express*

'Plenty of do-able recipes. ... all a huge success!' *Essentials*

'An indispensable guide for last-minute and everyday cooking – no kitchen should be without one.' *Four Shires*

'The author is a total expert at creating delicious food from very meagre shopping lists. Her tips and brilliant, simple recipes have been compiled into this great little book. Everyone can learn from this book – it's a brilliant resource, especially if you are trying to stick to a budget or are still finding your feet in the kitchen.' *easylivingmagazine.co.uk*

'I think it's a great buy.' *Uxbridge Gazette*

'I have to say, this is the first time I have ever read a cookery book from cover to cover in the space of a few days ... it's not just recipes, though there are plenty of those; but nuggets of wisdom about how to get children (and adults) to eat healthily without getting too fat, lots of humour and some apt quotations ... If anything is going to motivate me to change, this book will. In fact I can't wait! *Amazon VINE reviewer*

'A good starter basic for an inexperienced cook looking after a family on a budget and trying to steer clear of processed food and ready meals.' *www.tribune.ie*

'Buy this, bye stress with this fantastic cookbook, full of simple and nutritious recipes for family meals – ideal for those with a busy lifestyle.' *Prima*

'A handy little book full of easy ideas for family meals – straightforward, sustaining everyday food, quickly made with fresh ingredients, that will have your kids coming back for more. It's really useful and very definitely family-friendly.' *www.healthy-eating-made-easy.com/*

'Packed with great ideas for cost-conscious meals, packed lunches and extras like flapjacks and toffee apples. There's also some great advice on menu planning, with five weeks' worth of ideas that mean you won't have to cook the same meal twice during that time.' *Easy Cook Magazine*

£9.99 • ISBN 978-1-905862-15-3

"Good cooking is an art which is easily acquired. There are only a few basic processes, and once they are mastered, even elaborate dishes seem simple to produce. No cookbook can provide the spark of genius, but it can serve as a source of inspiration and information."

Fanny Farmer

Introduction

Whenever I'm asked about 'the right way' to shop, cook or eat, all I can say is I'm no expert, I only know what works for me. And as long as you're not living on takeaways and feeding your children a non-stop diet of processed ready meals and fizzy drinks, I don't think there are, strictly speaking, any wrong ways, just lots of different right ones.

The other question I'm often asked is where a certain recipe comes from, and usually all I can say to that is, I'm not sure, it was just an idea. In fact, I don't mind admitting that lots of my ideas were somebody else's idea first, which is why I never refer to any recipe as mine, however much it feels as if it belongs to me because I've cooked it so many times, or because I like to think my version is the best one.

Let's face it. Nobody's born with 200 failsafe recipes inside their head. Inspiration has to come from somewhere, and most recipes can be altered, adapted and updated to suit anyone and everyone, which is how it should be, and why so many old favourites manage to stay fresh and interesting no matter how many times they've been recycled.

In fact, recipe ideas are everywhere: on television and radio, in books, magazines and newspapers, even given away free in the supermarket, and yet some people still say it's not that easy to put a decent meal together. But mainly it's a state of mind; all you have to do is look at your options and find out what works for you.

Someone I know recently told me she can't face chopping onions so she uses ready-chopped frozen onions in all her cooking; that way she's got the beginnings of a meal in as little time as it takes to open a packet and warm some oil in a pan.

That's the beauty of cheat ingredients, whether you're using curry paste, instant gravy granules or ready-made salads. Anything that helps you get a home-made meal together has to be a good thing. It doesn't have to be cooked completely from scratch either. What's the point of having so much convenience if you can't cut corners and compromise? Surely all that matters is being able to produce something delicious and mostly nutritious that doesn't cost a small fortune or take too long to cook – and that you and your family will actually want to eat.

I also think we worry too much about fat grams, salt levels, different sugars, good fats and bad fats, calorie counting and eating five portions of fruit and vegetables every day, and I'm always coming across recipes for a 'healthy alternative' to chocolate cake, or 'guilt-free' fish and chips. But, to me, all fish and chips should be guilt free. Fish dipped in batter contains the same amount of nutrients as steamed fish. Potatoes are full of vitamins and minerals, whether they've been deep-fried or not. If you want a healthy alternative to chocolate cake, eat an apple, but if you really want the cake, eat that – and don't feel bad about it.

We all have to eat and even though cooking may not be fun all the time, it doesn't have to be a terrible chore either. One of my favourite quotes comes from Fran Lebowitz who apparently said: *'Food is an important part of a balanced diet.'* And I think that just about sums it up.

Good beginnings

STORE CUPBOARD INGREDIENTS

There's been a lot of talk lately about the advantages of stocking up on basic essentials and non-perishable items at home, but I still think it's worth repeating here simply because it's such a good point. In other words, if you've got a cupboard full of food to start with it's much easier to put a meal together in the evening, even when you're tired and really don't feel like cooking.

The list below may look very long but you don't have to buy the whole lot at once and even if you are starting from scratch, everything here is still very affordable and comparatively good value for money. Buying three or four different types of flour may seem a bit excessive if you're not used to it, but when you remember that flour is the basis for a huge variety of breads, pastries, cakes, biscuits, batters, toppings and sauces, a large bag costs around 75p (or less) in the supermarket and can last for weeks, it makes a bit more sense.

In any case, you'll soon get to know which items you use all the time and which ones you can do without altogether, then you can plan and shop accordingly – and start making your life easier.

TINS: Fish (sardines, salmon, tuna); **vegetables** (chopped tomatoes, plum tomatoes, sweetcorn, mushy peas, mixed); **fruit** (peaches, apples, pineapple, mixed); **beans** (baked, bortelli, cannellini, butter beans, broad beans, mixed); also **corned beef**, **coconut milk**, **black treacle**.

DRIED: Fruit (apricots, prunes, sultanas, raisins, cranberries, mixed); **lentils** and **pulses** (red lentils, green lentils, mung beans, yellow split peas, chickpeas); **rice*** (brown, basmati); **nuts** (peanuts, cashews, almonds, mixed); **seeds** (sesame, pumpkin, sunflower, mixed); **flour** (plain, self-raising, wholemeal, strong bread flour, gram flour – otherwise known as chickpea flour – cornflour); **sugar** (caster, soft brown); also **baking powder, dried yeast, suet, porridge oats, pasta, couscous, soup mix, salt, pepper, herbs** and **spices.**

* **NB:** avoid so-called 'easy cook' rice, which is more expensive and no easier to cook than any other type of rice. The only 'advantage' is that it supposedly takes a couple of minutes less cooking time – and I'm not even convinced of that.

BOTTLES: Oil (vegetable or corn oil, olive oil, sesame oil); **vinegar** (malt, cider, balsamic); also **lemon juice, lime juice, Worcestershire sauce, soy sauce, Tabasco sauce, sherry, honey, golden syrup.**

JARS: Mustard (English, French, Dijon); **pesto** (red and green); also **horseradish, sandwich pickle, chutney, jam.**

OTHER: Purées (tomato, garlic); also cartons of long-life **tomato juice** and **orange juice; stock cubes, gravy browning,** instant **gravy granules; Marmite** or **Vegemite.**

FRIDGE AND FREEZER

Lots of us buy pretty much the same dairy products every week according to what our own family's favourites are and many people regularly buy a much greater variety of cheeses and yoghurts than I've listed below; this is really just a rough guide to the most useful for those of you who want to keep to the minimum.

Generally, you can't beat fresh vegetables for texture and flavour, but it's also true that frozen vegetables are just as nutritious, and a few – peas and some beans, for instance – are actually better frozen. (You're also less likely to let frozen food get past its use-by date.) That said, some frozen fruit and vegetables aren't so good. Spinach is one example; I can't see the point of it when the fresh stuff is ready in about one minute and can be added straight to other dishes (stir-fries, casseroles and omelettes for example), whereas frozen spinach is soggy, lacks flavour and seems to me to take considerably longer to cook. Also, strawberries don't freeze well, nor does cabbage, and frozen pineapple is nowhere near as good in texture or sweetness as tinned.

FRESH: Cheese (Cheddar, Parmesan, Quark); **fats** (butter, Stork margarine, lard or Cookeen, the vegetarian alternative to lard); also **milk**, natural **yoghurt, eggs.**

FROZEN: Fish (white fish fillets, salmon or tuna fillets, prawns, fish fingers); **vegetables** (peas, French beans, broad beans, sweetcorn); **fruit** (mixed forest fruits, mixed summer fruits, raspberries, cranberries).

HERBS AND SPICES

I sometimes tried to grow herbs and other things in pots in the back garden when my kids were younger, but nothing could withstand the hailstorm of footballs and tennis balls for very long. In fact, the one and only thing that somehow managed to survive is a rosemary bush that I still use a lot, and which serves as a constant reminder that fresh herbs really are better than dried, and – in a ball-free zone – very easy to grow ...

Meanwhile, dried herbs and spices are infinitely better than none at all and still add a lot of depth and flavour to most sweet and savoury foods.

The herbs and spices listed here are the ones that crop up most regularly in the recipes in this book. Assume that the curry and chilli powder in each recipe will be medium unless stated otherwise, and just adapt whatever you happen to have (mild, medium or hot) to suit yourself, adding more or less of each one according to taste.

◆ **Ginger:** Warm and spicy: perfect in curries, stir-fries, cakes, biscuits and soups.

◆ **Curry powder/Chilli powder:** These tend to add heat rather than flavour (this is especially true of chilli powder) and ideally need to be combined with other spices to enhance the taste of the food.

◆ **Cumin powder/cumin seeds:** Boost the effect of curry and chilli powder and add their own flavour.

◆ **Garlic salt:** Good for meatball mixtures and marinades when you want the flavour without the hassle of peeling, chopping or crushing the bulb.

◆ **Onion salt:** Ditto.

◆ **Paprika:** Subtly different from **cayenne pepper**, which is more fiery where paprika is milder and sweeter. Use paprika for a subtle flavour and cayenne pepper when you want more heat.

◆ **Coriander:** Great in curries, Mexican dishes, carrot and other orange vegetable soups.

◆ **Garam masala:** A mixture – generally cinnamon, cumin, cloves, pepper, nutmeg and cardamom – used in a huge variety of curries. If you keep enough spices at home you can mix up your own versions of garam masala to suit yourself.

◆ **Mixed Spice:** Good in cakes and biscuits, and as an alternative to **Allspice** (which is similar but sharper; tasting more heavily of cloves) in some savoury dishes – stir-fries, for example.

◆ **Cinnamon:** Sweet and spicy, perfect with apples in cakes, puddings and biscuits.

◆ **Nutmeg:** Good with spinach, bananas, spicy cakes and biscuits.
◆ **Parsley:** Sprinkled over tomato, potato, egg, cheese and fish dishes.
◆ **Chives:** Omelettes, potato salad, vegetable dishes.
◆ **Rosemary:** roast lamb, shepherd's pie, some chicken dishes; also good with roast potatoes.
◆ **Sage:** Great with pork, sausages and onions; also home-made stuffing.
◆ **Tarragon:** Some fish and most chicken dishes.
◆ **Oregano:** Bolognese, tomato dishes and pasta sauces.
◆ **Herbes de Provence:** A good all-round substitute when you know you want to add a little flavour to something but you're not sure what to use.
◆ **Mixed herbs:** Ditto.

Chillies

If you buy chillies in packets in the supermarket the labels should give you all the information you need. In a nutshell, the little long, thin green ones are used in Asian curries; Scotch Bonnet chillies, which are small, round, crinkly and can be any colour from pale yellow or green to orangey red, are used in Caribbean cooking, while mixed red and green jalapenos are mostly for Mexican-style recipes.

As well as fresh chillies and dried spices you can also buy chilli flakes in jars in most supermarkets.

Stock

Chicken and turkey carcasses are perfect for making stock, as are beef, lamb, pork and gammon joints and knuckles. All you need to do is bring the bones to the boil in a pan of fresh, cold water with a bouquet garni, bay leaves, black peppercorns and a couple of onions and/or carrots if you have them. The stock should be skimmed to remove any fat from the surface after 2–3 hours, and can be re-boiled the next day, kept in the fridge for up to one week or frozen for up to three months.

Vegetable stock is also easy to make from a variety of peelings and leftover stalks, and needs only to be simmered for about half an hour. (However, Brussels sprouts have too strong a flavour and tend to overpower everything else so you're better off leaving them out, and don't use red cabbage leaves unless you want your finished stock to be blue.)

Fish stock can be made from scraps of fish with some onion or pale vegetable peelings, but never use fish bones; they make the stock taste bitter and render it completely useless.

Quantities

The quantities of vegetables and seasoning in lots of these recipes are approximate and can be adjusted any which way you like. (In some recipes specific quantities aren't given at all.)

Because I like recipes with lots of leeway I'm not very precise about quantities generally and only include them for one of the following reasons: as a starting point for anyone who hasn't cooked the dish before; because it's helpful to know in advance how many portions you can expect to make with a certain weight or volume of food or liquid, or in cases where the amount of any ingredient in the recipe will directly affect the end result.

All eggs are medium unless a recipe specifies another grade and, needless to say, to be able to judge a handful all you need is your own hand and a bit of common sense, not a certain-sized hand (as somebody once suggested to me – honestly). Similarly, where I've said a mug or a cup you'll know exactly what a regular mug or cup looks like.

Where a 'standard' tin is mentioned this refers to the average, most common size, although the weight or volume given on the tin could say 410 g, 400 ml or 14 oz. And where a recipe mentions just 'a tin' this either refers to the standard size, or it means the quantity simply doesn't matter so you can use any size tin you like.

I never give specific amounts of butter and oil for frying because everyone has their own idea of what's right. A generous amount of butter to me would be about 1 oz (25 g), but another person may use even less than that, whereas somebody else could easily double it, so err on the side of caution to start with; you can always add more as you go, but once you've got too much oil sloshing around in a pan full of food there's not much you can do about it. Also, I opt for butter and certain kinds of oil (or a combination of the two) in each recipe according to what feels right to me, but if you have a better idea and prefer to use different oil or another kind of fat altogether, that's fine.

Servings

I know it's usual to give a rough indication of how many people each recipe serves, but because this is a family cookbook you can safely assume that every recipe will serve at least four people – and usually more – unless stated otherwise.

Measuring

For some recipes – usually the puddings – you will have to weigh the ingredients, but once you know what an ounce (or 25 g) of something looks like, you'll probably find you can do without a set of scales most of the time and measure everything with a tablespoon. One tablespoon = 1 oz (25 g). (Use the same-sized spoon every time and you'll soon get the hang of it.)

I still think of everything in ounces, pounds and inches rather than metric, so although you shouldn't have problems with either system, there's the tiniest possibility that the imperial measurements will be slightly more accurate. And if you're still not sure about the size of something, fill a tin or pudding basin with flour and weigh that (e.g. a 2 lb loaf tin will hold 2 lb of flour), and for liquids fill the bowl or tin with water and pour it into a measuring jug.

Oven temperatures

The oven temperatures given here should at least be accurate enough for the recipes, and in most cases are ideal. In any case, as long as you're familiar with your own oven you'll soon be able to tell if you need to turn the temperature up or down a notch or two without making any drastic changes to the cooking times.

Equipment

Some people love kitchen gadgets and I can appreciate a gorgeous, expensive set of saucepans as much as the next person, but if you can't afford anything better than the bog standard basics, it won't make the slightest bit of difference to your cooking, believe me. It's certainly true that you're better off buying two or three good-quality knives than a whole set of cheap ones that don't cut anything properly (except your fingers) but all the mixing bowls, casserole dishes, saucepans, cake tins, measuring jugs, whisks, spatulas, spoons and other bits and pieces can be bought dirt cheap from the supermarket or pound shop.

An electric hand whisk is perfect for making cakes, among other things, while a food processor or blender (preferably 2 litre plus) is good for mixing, beating and liquidizing anything and everything. You should still be able to find these things for sale at around £5 for a hand whisk and £20 for a food processor. Hand blenders are also very useful, especially if you want to purée food for babies or make lots of soups and sauces. Finally, I should point out that in many of these recipes you could just as easily use a food processor instead of making dough or squishing meat mixtures together with your hands. I hardly ever do because I'd rather get my hands dirty and make less washing up, but the choice is yours.

"Tomatoes and oregano make it Italian; wine and tarragon make it French, sour cream makes it Russian, lemon and cinnamon make it Greek, Soy sauce makes it Chinese, garlic makes it good."

Alice May Brock

2
Mood food

CLASSICS

From modern classics like Pacific Pie and Creamy Pasta Bake to more traditional meals like Goulash or Stew and Dumplings, all the recipes in this section will be familiar to someone, depending on where they come from and the kind of food they were brought up on. I should also point out that, as with all the other recipes in this book, these dishes are neither 100% authentic nor completely 'wrong'; they're just variations of certain recipes the way I make them.

"It is more important to make classic dishes properly (which means deliciously, with the best available ingredients, following fundamental principles) than to keep trying to come up with new concoctions just for the sake of originality."

Julia Child

CHICKEN CHASSEUR

You can buy Chasseur sauce in jars or packet mixes in the supermarket, but it's almost as simple, and certainly more cost effective, to make at home.

Use whichever cut of chicken you like, but thighs are a cheaper option than breast meat and you can get away with a smaller quantity of any type of meat when it's served in a thick sauce. (If you haven't got white wine, use red, or even sherry will do.)

6 chicken thighs
Button mushrooms
Baby onions or shallots
1 tin of chopped tomatoes
³/₄ pint (450 ml) chicken stock
Glass of white wine
1 tbsp sugar
Tomato purée
Garlic purée
Tarragon
Oil
Salt & pepper
Butter

Method
1. Remove the chicken skin, wash and trim any fatty bits off the meat then season with salt and pepper. Peel and chop the onions, or leave them whole if they're small enough, ditto the mushrooms.
2. Warm a very little oil in a very large pan and brown the chicken thighs two or three at a time by cooking for a few minutes and turning once. (Don't put all the meat in the pan at the same time; if you do the chicken will just cook in its own steam without browning.)
3. Put the chicken thighs in a large casserole dish and sprinkle with tarragon.

4. Add a tablespoon of butter to the pan then fry the onions and mushrooms together for a few more minutes before putting them in the casserole dish with the chicken.

5. Add the stock, wine and chopped tomatoes to the pan with the sugar and a good squeeze each of tomato and garlic purée; stir well, bring to the boil and thicken the sauce with more tomato purée (or a little gravy browning or instant gravy granules) if necessary.

6. Cook in a preheated oven, Gas Mark 5 (190ºC) for about half an hour until the chicken is cooked through and the sauce is bubbling. Serve with potatoes or rice and extra vegetables or salad.

Tip

Don't chuck out tomatoes, even if they're slightly soft and wrinkly and past their best; make an alternative to sun dried tomatoes (kind of) by baking them in the oven. Keep covered in the fridge and use in meat and other tomato based sauces.

SHEPHERD'S PIE

Shepherd's Pie is a well-worn classic and there's no excuse really for printing a recipe that most people could make in their sleep, except it's one of my all-time favourites, so here it is again.

1 lb (450–500 g) minced lamb or beef
1 onion
1 clove of garlic
Mushrooms
1 carrot, grated

Frozen sweetcorn
1 lamb, beef or vegetable stock cube (or a teaspoon of Marmite)
1–2 tbsp tomato purée
1 heaped tbsp instant gravy granules
Dried rosemary
Potatoes: however many you think would make a serving of mash
for each person.
Milk
Grated cheese: approx 1 oz (25 g)

Method

1. Peel potatoes – or wash them and leave them in their skins if
    you prefer – then boil and mash in the usual way, adding butter,
    a splash of milk and the grated cheese to the finished mash.
2. Meanwhile, dry fry the meat in a very large pan over a moderate
    heat, breaking it up with a wooden spoon, while you get the
    vegetables ready.
3. Add the finely chopped onion, crushed garlic and mushrooms
    to the pan, and cook for a few minutes until the onions are soft
    and you can clearly see the meat's fatty juices.
4. Strain the fat off the meat then crumble in the stock cube (or
    a dessertspoonful of Marmite) and add the rosemary, tomato
    purée, grated carrot and as much frozen sweetcorn as you like;
    say a couple of handfuls.
5. Add the gravy granules to the pan with a little water and
    simmer for a few minutes.
6. Transfer the meat mixture to a large ovenproof dish and top
    with the mashed potatoes. Cook on Gas Mark 5 (190ºC) for
    roughly 20 minutes, or until the potatoes are brown and the
    gravy is bubbling.

> **Tip**
> Potatoes make one of the best toppings for pies and casseroles: mashed potatoes with added herbs and soft cheese or grated hard cheeses; or boiled potatoes cut into slices and dotted with butter.

FAGGOTS

Traditionally, faggots are wrapped in some kind of skin, rather like sausages, and poached in stock or gravy, which is what gives them that lovely soft texture, but these faggots are partly baked to stop them falling apart (without a skin), so they're soft in the middle and crisp on the outside.

Don't be put off by the ingredients – or the name – if you haven't tried these before. They're very tasty, and with 1lb of pork mince costing around £2 and 1 lb of lambs' liver at less than £1 in the supermarket, they're also very cheap.

(Wrap a rasher of streaky bacon around each faggot if you like, or leave them as they are.)

Makes 10 faggots
1 lb (500 g) pork mince
1 lb (500 g) lambs' liver
1 onion
2 oz (50 g) breadcrumbs
¾ pint (450 ml) stock
Mixed herbs
½ tsp cayenne pepper

Method

1. Prepare the liver in the usual way by rinsing in a colander under the cold tap and snipping off any little bits of skin or sinew with kitchen scissors.
2. Break up the mince in an ovenproof dish and mix with the roughly chopped liver and onion then pour on the stock, cover with a lid and bake in the oven for about 30 minutes.
3. Remove the cooked meat and onion from the stock and mince coarsely, either by putting it all through a mincer, or by pulsing in the food processor for a few seconds. (Don't overdo it and reduce the whole lot to slush.)
4. Add the breadcrumbs, herbs and cayenne pepper to the meat mixture and squish it all together so it's properly combined.
5. Form into cakes with your hands and place the faggots on a lightly oiled baking tray.
6. Bake in the oven on Gas Mark 5 (190°C) for another 30 minutes and serve with gravy, mashed potatoes and vegetables.

PORK SATAY

Needless to say, you can also make chicken or beef satay with this recipe, which can be cooked on the barbecue in summer or under the grill in winter.

It doesn't matter whether you use metal or wooden skewers, but if you use wooden ones soak them in cold water for a couple of hours then wipe them over with a little oil first to stop them charring – or igniting – on the barbecue. (Alternatively, you could cook the pork still in its marinade in a covered casserole dish in the oven and serve it on a bed of rice.)

2 lb (1 kg) lean pork fillet
2 tbsp smooth peanut butter
2 tbsp soy sauce
½ tin of coconut milk
2 tsp black treacle
1 tsp each of mustard seeds, cumin seeds, 5 Spice, coriander, garlic salt, onion salt
½ tsp chilli powder
Lemon juice

Method
1. Crush the mustard and cumin seeds (put them between 2 pieces of greaseproof paper and press down hard with a rolling pin a few times if you haven't got a pestle and mortar) and put them in a bowl with the rest of the ingredients – except the pork – then beat everything together with a fork or a wooden spoon to make a smooth marinade.
2. Trim excess fat from the pork and cut the meat into cubes with a pair of kitchen scissors then put the meat in a casserole dish, mix well with the marinade, cover and keep in the fridge for about 4 hours.
3. Remove the pork from the marinade, set the sauce to one side, and thread the meat onto metal or wooden skewers. Grill or barbecue the pork for 10–15 minutes, turning frequently.
4. Meanwhile, warm the marinade over a gentle heat, stirring occasionally, and serve separately as a dipping sauce with the pork satay, a side dish of rice and an assortment of *crudités*. Cucumber and carrot sticks, spring onions, strips of red and green pepper are all good.

LIVER CASSEROLE

Lots of people are put off liver because they remember being forced to eat it as a child, usually at school, and it's true that in its raw state, or just fried, it's really not very nice – calves' liver excepted.

The answer lies in the preparation. Spend a few minutes removing the skin and trimming the nasty bits away then cook the liver in a nice sauce with more appealing ingredients and you've got a result. Best of all, liver is packed with protein and it's still dirt cheap.

2 packets of liver
½ lb (225 g) of bacon
Onions
Mushrooms
½ pint (250 ml) gravy
1 tin chopped tomatoes
Tomato purée
Mustard (English or French)
Flour
Salt & pepper
Oil

Method
1. Wash the liver in a colander under cold running water then trim carefully, cut into small pieces and coat well in the seasoned flour.
2. Snip the bacon into small pieces and get rid of any rind or excess fat.
3. Chop and slice the onions and mushrooms while you warm some oil in a large frying pan. Start cooking the onions first, adding the mushrooms after a couple of minutes, and when

you think they're ready transfer to a large casserole dish.

4. Fry the liver and bacon pieces together over a high heat, adding a little more oil to the pan first, if necessary, then add to the casserole with the onions and mushrooms.

5. Empty the tin of chopped tomatoes into the pan and make up ½ pint (250 ml) of instant gravy in a measuring jug. Add the gravy to the pan with about one tablespoon of tomato purée and a little mustard, stir well and allow to warm through for a couple of minutes before pouring into the casserole dish.

6. Cover with a lid and cook in the oven, Gas Mark 5 (190°C) for 10–15 minutes.

RAISED PORK PIE

This is so old-fashioned there are records of this recipe dating back to the 15th century, meaning raised pork pies were absolutely ancient hundreds of years before Mrs Beeton's time, so it's a pity our experience of pork pies tends to be limited to the very pink and unnatural mass-produced shop-bought variety today.

Originally, raised pork pies were so called because the pastry was pulled up or raised around a jar or a thick collar of greaseproof paper to get its shape, and some people, including my sister-in-law Claire (who gave me her recipe) still make them this way; far too demanding for people like me who only have as much dexterity and patience as it takes to fill and unload a spring-release cake tin.

You can't knock one up in a few minutes flat either – there's a long cooking and waiting time – but home-made pork pies are actually very easy to make, and so much better than the aforementioned pink ones that they're definitely worth doing occasionally, especially as they're also pretty economical if you think about it. The amount of meat in this recipe, roughly 3 lb

(1.5 kg), costs around £6; the other ingredients are cheap store cupboard items, and the result is a huge, impressive-looking pie, made in an 8–9 inch (20.5 cm) tin, which is enough to feed at least a dozen people.

You can either use boneless leg or shoulder of pork cut into cubes, or minced pork and good-quality sausages, which could be pork and herb, pork and apple, Cumberland or Lincolnshire, or a combination of any of these, but there's no point in making a home-made pie with value sausages or cheap sausagemeat. You may as well not bother.

Finally, although all traditional pork pie recipes involve making aspic for pouring into the pie at the end, I can't see the point of making jellied stock or, heaven forbid, boiling up veal bones for the real thing, which adds at least two more stages to the method, makes the pastry soggier than it needs to be and contributes very little to the whole pork pie eating experience since I've never met anyone who doesn't immediately remove the jelly and leave it on the side of their plate. (Although admittedly, home-made jelly is a lot nicer than the thick, white glutinous stuff in shop-bought pies.)

Anyway, I've included the jelly-making bit just in case, so put it in or leave it out – it's up to you.

For the pastry
1lb (500 g) plain flour
1 level tbsp salt
4 oz (100 g) lard (or Trex)
½ pint (250 ml) water

For the filling
1 lb (500 g) minced pork
2 packets x 6 good-quality sausages, total 2 lb (1 kg)
1 big tsp each of sage, parsley, marjoram, nutmeg, onion salt and
    black pepper
½ tsp cayenne pepper

1 egg, beaten

For the jelly
1 stock cube
1 bouquet garni
1 bay leaf
1 sachet of gelatine
½ pint (250 ml) boiling water

Method
1. Put ½ pint (250 ml) of water and the fat into a small saucepan
    and bring to the boil; meanwhile sift the flour and salt into a
    large mixing bowl and make a well in the centre.
2. Once the fat has melted and the water has just reached boiling
    point, pour the liquid into the well and quickly beat in the
    flour with a wooden spoon to make a dough. (Don't worry if
    the dough looks a bit dry and doesn't come together perfectly
    at this stage; it will once you start working it by hand.)
3. Start pinching the dough together with your fingers (do it
    carefully, it's still very hot) and knead well until it becomes a
    smooth, shiny ball. Cover the dough with a damp cloth or cling
    film and leave in a warm place to rest for about half an hour.
4. If you're making the jelly, dissolve the stock cube in ½ pint
    (250 ml) of boiling water in a measuring jug at this stage, add
    a bay leaf and a bouquet garni bag and leave to cool for about

half an hour before covering and keeping in the fridge.

5. While you're waiting for the dough, preheat the oven to Gas Mark 4–5 (180–190ºC) and baseline the tin with greaseproof paper, lightly oiling the whole inside of the tin. Prepare the meat mixture by squeezing the sausages out of their skins and mixing them with the minced pork, herbs and spices, then squishing it all together with your hands.

6. Roll out $^2/_3$ of the dough on a lightly floured surface till it makes a rough, thick circle slightly larger than the base of the tin. Put the circle of dough in the tin and raise it up the sides of the tin by gently pressing and stretching the dough from the centre, outwards and upwards.

7. Fill the pie with the meat mixture in a dome shape to give the finished pie a more pleasing appearance than if it was just flat across the top.

8. Roll out the remaining $^1/_3$ of the dough into a rough circle about the same size as the first one to make the lid. Cover the pie with the lid, trimming the lid into shape and firmly pinching the edges and sides of the pastry together with your thumb and forefinger all the way round to make a crust.

9. Use the pastry trimmings to decorate the pie by cutting out leaves with a small sharp knife, or making any shapes you like with pastry cutters. Make a hole about the size of a pencil in the centre of the pie if you're making jelly later and glaze the pastry with the beaten egg.

10. Bake the pie on Gas Mark 5–6 (190–200ºC) for about half an hour, then turn the oven down to Gas Mark 3–4 (170–180ºC), cover loosely with foil and bake for another $2^1/_2$ hours until the pastry is a deep golden brown.

11. Release the spring immediately and remove the ring leaving the pie on the base to cool down for about 1 hour. Put the pie in the fridge as soon as you can and leave for at least 4 hours and preferably overnight to become completely cold.

To make the jelly

It's very important that the jelly is cold when you pour it into the pie; if it isn't the hot stock will warm the meat up just enough to create a haven for bacteria. Don't try and pour warm jelly into a still warm pie either; the pastry will soak it all up and turn to mush. And although you're making ½ pint (250 ml) of stock you won't need this much so pour it into the pie really slowly.

1. Remove the bouquet garni and bay leaves from the stock and heat it thoroughly, either in the microwave or by bringing it to boiling point in a small saucepan.
2. Sprinkle about ⅔ of a sachet of gelatine into the boiling hot stock, whisking with a fork for about a minute until you're sure the powder has dissolved.
3. Put the stock into a very big oven dish or similar; anything with a large surface area that will cool the stock right down in a matter of minutes so it's completely cold while it's still in liquid form. (If you leave it to cool slowly the jelly will set.)
4. Transfer the stock back into the measuring jug and pour slowly and carefully through the hole in the middle of the pastry.
5. Refrigerate the pork pie for at least another 2 or 3 hours then remove the base of the tin and the layer of greaseproof and stand the pie on a plate.
6. Keep the pork pie in the fridge and use within one week.

CHICKEN CORDON BLEU

Quark mixed with herbs and garlic makes a good low fat alternative to Emmental or other hard cheeses.

4 chicken breast fillets
4 slices of lean ham
Quark
Garlic salt
Herbes de Provence
4–6 oz (100–150g) breadcrumbs
1 egg
Splash of milk
Flour
Oil

Method

1. Remove the skin from the chicken, rinse and dry the meat thoroughly and trim any little fatty bits. (If the fillets are *very* large, cut them in half.) With a very sharp knife, slice through the middle of each piece of chicken about ³⁄₄ of the way through.
2. Open out the chicken pieces and put in the ham.
3. Mix about ³⁄₄ of the tub of Quark with garlic salt and herbs (according to taste) then roughly spread the cheese over the ham and fold the chicken making sure the fillings are tucked neatly inside.
4. Spread the breadcrumbs out on a large plate or tray. Put a couple of tablespoons of flour on another plate and mix the beaten egg with a big splash of milk in a fairly large, shallow bowl.
5. Warm about an inch (2 cm) of oil in a large pan and preheat the oven to Gas Mark 6 (200°C) while you dust the chicken pieces

with a little flour then dip them first in the beaten egg mixture before covering completely in breadcrumbs.

6. As soon as the oil is hot enough – i.e. a small piece of bread turns brown in about half a minute – put the chicken fillets in the pan two at a time and fry for a few minutes until crisp and golden, turning once.

7. Finish cooking the chicken in the oven for about 15 minutes, depending on size, and serve with fried potatoes, or rice and salad.

CHICKEN KIEV

Try making a paste with olive oil rather than stuffing the chicken with garlic butter in the usual way; that way you get nice moist chicken and just as much flavour without so much grease. If you'd rather have garlic butter though, mix the same amount of garlic, onion salt and parsley with roughly 2 oz (50 g) of butter.

Use regular breadcrumbs instead of biscuit crumbs if you prefer, or a mixture of both.

4 chicken breast fillets
2 cloves of garlic
2 tsp salt
2 tsp onion or celery salt
2 tsp parsley
1½ tbsp olive oil
8 cream crackers
2–3 handfuls of cornflakes
1 egg
Splash of milk
Flour

Method

1. Remove the skin from the chicken, rinse and dry the meat thoroughly and trim any little fatty bits. (If the fillets are *very* large, cut them in half.) With a very sharp knife, slice through the middle of each piece of chicken about ³/₄ of the way through.

2. In a small bowl, crush the garlic and mix to a paste with the salt, onion or celery salt, parsley and olive oil.

3. Whiz the crackers and cornflakes in a food processor, or put the whole lot in a large food bag and crush with a rolling pin or other heavy object, then tip the biscuit crumbs onto a dinner plate or shallow tray. Put a couple of tablespoons of flour on another plate and mix the beaten egg with a big splash of milk in a fairly large, shallow bowl.

4. Warm about an inch (2 cm) of oil in a large pan and preheat the oven to Gas Mark 6 (200ºC) while you spread the garlic paste (or garlic butter) in the middle of each piece of chicken.

5. Dust the chicken pieces with a little flour then dip first in the beaten egg mixture before covering completely in biscuit crumbs.

6. As soon as the oil is hot enough – i.e. a small piece of bread turns brown in about half a minute – put the chicken fillets in the pan two or three at a time and fry for a few minutes until crisp and golden.

7. Finish cooking the chicken in the oven for about 15 minutes, depending on size, and serve with fried potatoes, or rice and salad.

GOULASH

Maybe there's no such thing as a classic goulash because the ingredients vary considerably from one region to another according to the country of origin – Hungary and Austria most typically.

In fact, veal is traditionally used in the majority of goulash recipes, but apart from any principles you may have about eating veal, it's expensive and not particularly accessible, so I make mine with stewing or braising steak instead.

2 lb+ (at least 1 kg) stewing steak
Onions
Mushrooms
2 or 3 carrots
1 red pepper
1 green pepper
2 tbsp flour
2 tbsp paprika
1 tbsp sugar
1 level tsp cayenne pepper
1–1½ pints (600–850 ml) stock
½ glass white wine (or red, or sherry)
Worcestershire sauce
Tomato purée
Salt & pepper
Oil
Butter

Method
1. Warm some oil in a very large pan, trim any excess fat off the meat (there shouldn't be much in any case), preheat the oven to Gas Mark 2 (160ºC) and prepare and roughly chop the vegetables.
2. Season the meat with a very little salt and some pepper then fry over a high heat a few pieces at a time to seal and brown it quickly.
3. Put the cooked meat into a large casserole dish, discard any liquid left in the pan then add a little more oil or some butter (or some of each) and fry the carrots, peppers and onion for a few

minutes until they soften up a bit and brown slightly. Add the mushrooms to the pan and fry for another couple of minutes.

4. Turn the heat right down, sift in the paprika, cayenne pepper and flour and cook for another minute, stirring well.

5. Make the stock, add a couple of dashes of Worcestershire Sauce, a tablespoon of sugar and plenty of tomato purée then pour the stock and ½ glass of wine or sherry into the pan, stirring again.

6. Pour the stock and vegetables over the meat in the casserole dish and cook in a low oven for 2 ½–3 hours until the meat is very tender. Serve with mashed potatoes and green vegetables.

Tip

No need to wash red meat, just snip off any excess fat, season and use straight from the packet. (If you really *have* to rinse it first, dry it thoroughly or the meat won't seal well in the pan and the end result will be dry.)

STEW & DUMPLINGS

Irish stew is traditionally made with lamb and potatoes, whereas English stews tend to leave out the potatoes and have dumplings instead. This stew has both because I don't like giving up one for the other, but either beef or lamb will do so use whichever one you prefer.

Also, Irish stew includes pearl barley which I've left out here, but which could easily be added with the vegetables straight from the packet, or blanched in boiling water first according to the instructions on the box.

2 lb (1 kg) lamb neck fillet or stewing beef
4 large potatoes
2 turnips

1–2 onions
Carrots
1½ pints (850 ml) lamb or beef stock
1–2 tbsp plain or gram flour
1 tsp gravy browning mixed with ¼ mug of cold water
Black pepper
Lard or oil

For the dumplings
4 tbsp self-raising flour
2 tbsp suet
½ tsp salt
1 tbsp Herbes de Provence or mixed herbs
½ mug of cold water

Method
1. Trim the meat and season with a little black pepper while you warm some lard or oil in a very large pan and preheat the oven to Gas Mark 2–3 (160–170ºC).
2. Slice the onions and chop the vegetables into roughly same-size pieces. (Not too small though or they'll turn to mush in the oven.)
3. Seal the meat in the hot oil as quickly as you can and transfer to a large casserole dish.
4. Fry the onions, potatoes, turnips and carrots together, stir in the flour and cook for another couple of minutes before adding the vegetables to the casserole with the meat.
5. Make 1½ pints (850 ml) of stock with 1 stock cube and mix 1 big teaspoon of gravy browning in about ¼ mug of cold water.
6. Stir the gravy mixture into the stock then pour the liquid over the meat and vegetables.
7. Cover with a lid and cook in a slow oven for about 3 hours, or until the meat is completely tender.

8. Make the dumplings by mixing the flour, salt, suet and herbs together, gradually adding the cold water to make a soft but not too sticky dough.
9. Form the dough into very small dumplings and place on top of the stew.
10. Cook the stew for another 20 minutes or so without the lid, until the dumplings are risen and slightly golden.

SWEET & SOUR PORK

Make sweet and sour with seedless jam instead of sugar. This works well with cuts of pork that require longer cooking.

6 large pork fillets (or similar)
2 tbsp seedless jam (apricot, raspberry, strawberry or plum)
2 tbsp tomato purée
2 tbsp soy sauce
2 tbsp water
2 tsp mustard
2 tsp vinegar

Method
1. Wrap the pork in a parcel of foil inside a large ovenproof dish and bake in a low oven, Gas Mark 2–3 (160–170ºC) for about an hour.
2. Meanwhile, put the rest of the ingredients in a small bowl or measuring jug and mix together with a fork to make the sweet and sour sauce.
3. Remove the foil and place the pieces of pork side by side in the dish, coat well with the sauce and turn the oven up to Gas Mark 5 (190ºC).
4. Cook for about 20 minutes, turning once.
5. Serve with mashed or small roast potatoes and mixed vegetables.

Tip

King Edwards make perfect roast potatoes: parboil the potatoes and let them simmer for about five minutes, then strain the water off and bash the potatoes up a bit by giving them two or three good shakes in the saucepan with the lid on. When you put the potatoes into very hot oil or lard the soft outside absorbs some of the fat; that's what makes them lovely and crisp.

MUTTON DRESSED AS LAMB

Mutton is meant to be making a comeback as a more affordable alternative to lamb, but I can't see this happening when you don't often come across it in the supermarket, and most butchers I've asked say they have to order it in on request – although you'll almost certainly find mutton in halal butcher's shops.

Not only that, mutton can actually cost more than a good, cheap cut of lamb, which is a shame, because with the usual slow-cooking rule that applies to all but the most expensive cuts of meat, mutton can be just as tasty, with a texture and flavour of its own.

2 lb (1 kg) mutton
2 parsnips
1 turnip (or 2–3 small)
1 onion
Carrots
2 pints (1 litre) beef or lamb stock
1 glass of sherry
2–3 sprigs of rosemary (or 1 tbsp dried)

½ bunch of mint (or 1 tbsp dried)
1 tbsp sugar
Balsamic vinegar
Oil or lard

Method
1. Warm the oil or lard in a large saucepan while you trim and cut up the meat into roughly same-size pieces and prepare the vegetables in the same way.
2. Brown the meat in the hot fat as quickly as you can, transferring to a very large casserole or ovenproof dish as you go.
3. Put the rosemary on top of the meat – if using fresh, snip most of the leaves off but put the stalks in too; you can take them out later – and fry the vegetables for a few minutes, adding more oil to the pan as and when you need to.
4. Put the vegetables in a layer on top of the meat but don't mix them in with the meat; you'll need to remove them later, once the casserole is cooked, to make a sauce.
5. Make 2 pints (1 litre) of stock with 2 stock cubes, add the sherry and pour the liquid over the casserole. Cover with a lid and cook in a very low oven, Gas Mark 1–2 (150–160°C) for at least 3–3½ hours or until the meat is very tender.
6. Use a large serving spoon or ladle to remove the vegetables and most of the stock from the casserole and blend the whole lot together in a liquidizer or food processor to make a purée, keeping the meat warm at the same time.
7. Mix the mint, sugar and balsamic vinegar into the vegetable purée; remove the rosemary stalks from the casserole and stir the purée into the meat. Adjust the seasoning and consistency of the sauce and serve with roast or mashed potatoes, or rice.

Tip
If you buy a big bundle of fresh herbs and know you won't be able to use it up before it starts wilting, put what you don't need immediately in a sealed food bag and freeze.

GROUNDNUT TURKEY STEW

You can get at least ½ lb (225 g) of meat from a turkey drumstick that costs around £1.25 in the supermarket, so as long as you're not resigned to buying nothing but free range meat and poultry, turkey drumsticks are one of the cheapest options going.

Depending on what you're making, it's sometimes easier to cook your turkey drumstick whole and carve the meat off afterwards (using the bone to make stock) but for this recipe you need chopped raw meat, so cut the turkey away from the bone with a pair of kitchen scissors.

1–1½ lb (450–675 g) turkey
2 onions
2 cloves of garlic
1 orange or yellow pepper
½ lb (225 g) monkey nuts (or shelled peanuts)
1pint (500 ml) chicken stock
1 tin of chopped tomatoes
1 tbsp tomato purée
1 tbsp peanut butter
1 tsp cayenne pepper
Salt & pepper
Oil

Method

1. Heat some oil in a very large pan and fry the chopped onions, pepper and garlic for a few minutes until just soft.
2. Mix the fried vegetables with the peanuts and stock and whiz the whole lot in a blender or food processor for a minute until it's fairly smooth.
3. Meanwhile, warm some more oil in the same pan you used to cook the vegetables then fry the chopped turkey, quickly browning the meat on all sides.
4. Add the vegetable and peanut mixture to the pan with the meat followed by the chopped tomatoes, tomato purée, peanut butter and cayenne pepper.
5. Bring to the boil, stirring frequently, then turn the heat down and simmer the stew for about 45 minutes until the meat is tender.
6. Adjust the flavour and consistency with salt and pepper, extra cayenne pepper or Tabasco sauce for more heat, a little more tomato purée or peanut butter for thickness, or more stock to thin the sauce down.
7. Serve with plain boiled rice.

BEAN & FRANKFURTER RAGOUT

This is a very basic bean stew, which would be a bit boring without the addition of the frankfurters and cider to liven it up. (Still very cheap though.)

2 large packets of frankfurters
½ lb (225 g) dried red kidney beans
½ lb (225 g) dried haricot beans or chickpeas

1 red onion
Mushrooms
1 bottle of cider (330 ml)
2 tbsp tomato purée
1 tbsp cornflour
½ pint (250 ml) cold water
2 tsp chilli powder
Oil

Method

1. Soak the beans overnight then drain, rinse well under cold running water and put in a large pan with enough water to cover the beans completely.
2. Bring to the boil then boil rapidly for 15–20 minutes before draining the beans and rinsing in fresh cold running water again.
3. Meanwhile, fry the sliced onion and mushrooms in a large pan or flameproof casserole; mix the cornflour with the cold water then add to the pan with the cider, tomato purée and chilli powder.
4. Stir well and bring the liquid to the boil, then add the beans, cover with a lid and cook the ragout in a slow oven, Gas Mark 3 (170ºC) for 2–2½ hours until the beans are tender. (Check a couple of times throughout the cooking time and stir the ragout to stop the sauce sticking to the bottom of the pan.)
5. As soon as the beans are done, cut the frankfurters into thick slices diagonally and mix into the casserole, adding a little water if the sauce is too thick.
6. Cook for another 5 minutes. Serve with mashed or fried potatoes.

PACIFIC PIE

Like Pasta Bake, Pacific Pie is now something of a modern classic. Both meals are perfect for those times when you can't face proper cooking, and it also helps that you get to crush up lots of crisps, accidentally tearing open more bags than you need in the process, which is always a good thing.

There are no rules really; a couple of tins of fish and a sauce made from any combination of yoghurt, mayonnaise, condensed soup, crème fraîche and tomato purée with tinned or leftover vegetables and a cheesy, crunchy topping are all you need.

2 tins of salmon or tuna
1 tin of sweetcorn
1 tin of chopped tomatoes
Spinach
Natural yoghurt
Lemon juice
Grated cheese
Ready salted crisps
Salt & pepper

Method
1. Preheat the oven to Gas Mark 6 (200°C).
2. Wash and tear up the spinach; drain the tins of fish and sweetcorn then put everything in an ovenproof dish and add lemon juice, salt and pepper according to taste.
3. Add the chopped tomatoes and a couple of spoonfuls of yoghurt with whatever else you're using and mix it all up.
4. Crush the crisps and sprinkle on the top of the pie with lots of grated cheese. Bake in a hot oven for about 10 minutes.

CREAMY PASTA BAKE

I wouldn't normally precook the pasta for an oven-baked dish; pasta cooked twice is too starchy and rubbery, and cooking what should be a basic one-step recipe in two stages defeats the object of the exercise for me. That said, you only have to leave the pasta to stand in a pan of boiling water for as long as it takes to make a two-minute sauce, which doesn't really count as cooking, and the result is another perfect pasta bake in the space of half an hour; very tasty and easy to make.

As with all pasta bakes you can swap the ingredients around to suit yourself and, for an even quicker option, make the sauce with a tin of condensed soup diluted with a pint (500 ml) of milk – chicken, mushroom or asparagus are all good – and use tinned vegetables instead of frying onions and mushrooms at the beginning.

Pasta shapes
2 red onions
Mushrooms
Chorizo sausage
2 oz (50 g) butter or margarine
2tbsp flour
1 pint (500 ml) milk
Grated Cheddar or mozzarella (or a mixture of both)
Black pepper
Oil or butter

Method

1. Warm about 2 oz (50 g) of butter in a large pan, fry the chopped mushrooms and onions for a few minutes until the

onions are golden, then turn the heat right down.

2. Meanwhile, cut the chorizo sausage into small pieces.

3. Bring a saucepan of slightly salted water to the boil then turn the heat off, add the pasta to the pan (one or two handfuls per person), cover with a lid and leave to stand while you make the quick sauce.

4. Sift 2 tablespoons of flour into the pan with the fried mushrooms and onions, stir well and cook for about a minute.

5. Gradually pour the milk into the pan, stirring all the time, then turn the heat up and cook for a couple more minutes until you have a smooth, fairly thin sauce (whisk any lumps out with a fork or a small hand whisk). Season the sauce with black pepper.

6. Drain the pasta and transfer to a large ovenproof dish with the chorizo. Pour over the sauce and mix everything together thoroughly.

7. Sprinkle with plenty of grated cheese and bake in the oven on Gas Mark 4 (180ºC) for 15–20 minutes.

SPAM FRITTERS

When I first thought of making Spam Fritters for this book, every time I suggested it to someone they were horrified, which is why I had to put them in.

I must admit that until now I hadn't eaten Spam in any shape or form since I was at school, and I can't find anyone else who admits to eating it either, but tins of Spam are on the shelves in every supermarket so *somebody* out there must like it. Maybe Spam is another one of those secret vices, like Pot Noodle and tinned spaghetti hoops (see also Trifle and Butterscotch Crunch in Chapter 5, 'Something Sweet'), but because Spam is made from around 90% pork it's a pretty good source of protein in addition to being – I hate to say it – quite tasty.

In fact, the worst thing I can say about Spam is that, unbelievably, it's even harder to get out of the tin than corned beef, so perhaps if the packaging wasn't potentially so hazardous and liable to cut your fingers off, even more people would eat it.

The batter in this recipe is very light and crisp so the fritters won't be too oily. One or two small Spam fritters will easily feed a child and you'll get eight from one tin of Spam. (This amount of batter is more than enough for two tins.)

1 or 2 tins of Spam
4 tbsp plain flour
1–2 tbsp cornflour
½ pint (250 ml) cider
Oil

Method
1. Sift the flours together into a bowl and make a well in the centre; pour the cider into the well and gradually whisk in the flour to make a fairly thin, frothy batter.
2. Cut the Spam into 4 thick slices and cut each slice in half to make 8 small squares.
3. Warm enough oil in a large pan to just cover the fritters. Once the oil is hot enough, use a fork to dunk the fritters in batter then put them into the pan and fry for a very few minutes until the batter is crisp and just golden. Serve with baked beans and chips (what else?).

"I cook with wine, sometimes I even add it to the food."

W.C. Fields

COMFORT FOOD

There's a big difference between shop-bought junk food that's high in calories and low in nutrients, and the kind of relatively healthy, home-made comfort foods that most people crave occasionally – or even quite often – but which still contain a hefty dose of vitamins and minerals, and tend to be eaten with lots of vegetables and other low fat foods anyway ...

So don't be put off by dire warnings about the dangers of eating stodge and suet puddings. One of the best things about pies and pastries (apart from the taste, obviously) is that a little goes a long way, and you're far more likely to pick your way through a tin of biscuits on a cold winter evening if you force yourself to eat a cottage cheese salad for dinner when what you really wanted was pie and mash ...

CHIP SHOP CURRY SAUCE

If you thought nothing could beat a good chip shop curry sauce, think again. The home-made version is better. I put celery in mine because it leaves the sauce with a slightly crunchy texture even after the sauce has been blended, which I like, but if you want a smoother sauce, leave out the celery and put in extra apples.

And if my memory serves me right, I'm sure I've come across sultanas in chip shop curry sauce before, so there's no reason why you couldn't add some here if you like sultanas and want a bit more sweetness.

These quantities make enough for at least six very large servings of sauce.

1 big tbsp curry powder
2 tsp cumin

2 tsp cinnamon

2 tsp allspice

1 onion

3 apples

2–3 celery sticks

2–3 carrots

2 tbsp gram or plain flour

½ tube tomato purée

1 pint (500 ml) cold water

2 tsp gravy browning

1 tsp salt

1 tsp sugar

Oil

Method

1. Warm some oil in a very large pan while you peel and roughly chop the onion, celery and carrots and, finally, peel, core and cut up the apples. (Do the apples last to stop them going brown.)

2. Mix the curry powder, cumin, cinnamon and allspice together and add the spices to the hot oil in the pan, followed by the vegetables and fruit.

3. Stir well and cook over a low heat for a few minutes until the onion has softened a bit then sift in the flour and cook for another minute or two.

4. Meanwhile, put 2 tsp of gravy browning in a cup with a little of the water from the 1 pint (500 ml) and mix well with a teaspoon to make sure there are no lumps.

5. Pour the rest of the water into the pan and bring to the boil, stirring occasionally.

6. As soon as the water is hot, slowly pour the gravy browning into the pan and keep stirring.

7. Finally, add the tomato purée, sugar and salt, cover the pan with a lid and leave the sauce to simmer for 20–30 minutes. Blend the finished sauce and adjust the seasoning with a very little salt and pepper if you think you need to.
8. Serve with chips. Also good with sausages or chicken and rice.

CHIPS

Greasy French fries from fast food outlets deserve their bad reputation but home-made chips, chip shop chips, and even oven chips don't. So what if one portion of chips uses up half your daily fat allowance? I don't see why that should be a problem when a bag of chips is a meal in itself and once you've eaten them you still have the other half of your daily fat allowance left …

Chips are often condemned as the most offensive 'unhealthy' food of all, and while I agree that thin, soggy, oily chips are no good for children or anyone else, chunky chips that were deep fried in very hot oil so the nutrients are sealed in are actually a lot healthier and tastier than boiled potatoes that lose most of their vitamins in the water. My advice would be, tempt your children with chips and they're far more likely to eat the other vegetables on their plate without complaining. Honestly. It always worked in my house.

In fact, chips are the ultimate comfort food – with or without ketchup, mayonnaise, salad cream, or curry sauce – so forget about calorie counting and fat grams for once, stop thinking of them as 'an occasional treat', which is the advice given in just about every article I've ever read on the subject of 'healthy eating', and make chips a regular part of your diet. They're full of vitamins, taste good and fill you up without making you fat, and you can't ask for much more than that.

Home-made deep-fried chips: Maris Pipers are ideal. Serve with anything and everything.

1. Peel the potatoes, cut into chips, roughly ½ in (1.25 cm) thick, and rinse well in cold running water for about 10 seconds.
2. Allow the chips to drain while you heat the oil, making sure you've got rid of every last drop of water by blotting with an old, clean tea towel or kitchen roll. (When a cube of stale bread dropped into the oil turns golden within seconds, the oil is hot enough.)
3. If you have a chip basket big enough, use that, otherwise cook the chips loose, lowering them into the hot oil as carefully as you can.
4. Cover with a lid and check them often; they should be ready in about 20 minutes.

Home-made oven-baked chips: Sprinkle with salt, or any kind of ready mixed seasoning from a jar, or just leave plain.

1. Peel potatoes and cut into large chunks in the usual way while you preheat the oven to Gas Mark 7 (220ºC).
2. Pour a few tablespoons of oil onto a large baking tray or roasting dish, add the chips and use your hands to mix and coat with the oil.
3. Bake in the oven for 20–30 minutes, shaking the tray halfway through the cooking time.

New potato chips: Serve with fish or cold meat and salad.

1. Wash the potatoes in cold water; don't peel, leave them in their skins and dry thoroughly. Cut into halves or quarters depending on size.
2. Heat enough oil in a very large pan to completely submerge the potatoes and deep fry for roughly 15 minutes, or until crisp and golden brown on the outside, soft on the inside.
3. Drain on kitchen paper.

Plantain chips: Serve with any spicy food and a cool yoghurt dressing.

1. Peel the plantain with a sharp knife, cut each one in half then each half into quarters to make long chips. Deep fry or bake the plantain chips in the same way as home-made potato chips.

Mixed root vegetable chips: Mix up parsnips, turnips, potatoes and sweet potatoes and serve with onion marmalade, or sausages and tomato ketchup or brown sauce.

1. Peel and cut all the vegetables into fairly large, same-size chunks.
2. Simmer the potatoes in boiling water for a couple of minutes while you warm enough oil in a large pan to submerge the chips completely.
3. Strain the potatoes thoroughly and mix with the other vegetables.
4. Deep fry for about 15 minutes until golden brown and drain on kitchen paper.

PIE & MASH & LIQUOR

There are only a handful of pie and mash shops left these days, which is a great pity when there are so many vile burger bars and greasy fried chicken shops to choose from.

Anyway, even if pies go further out of fashion than they are now, you can still make them at home. I nearly always make mine with shortcrust pastry, but use ready-made puff pastry if you prefer. Either way, these little pies can be made in advance and kept in the fridge for a couple of days.

The other point I should make is that although the tin I use is meant to be a Yorkshire pudding tin, it's actually about the same size as an extra large muffin tin (I've also seen much bigger Yorkshire pudding tins than mine) but as long as the holes in the tin are deep enough and the tin looks about right to you, don't worry too much about the size, it should be fine.

You should get between 6 and 10 pies from the quantities in the recipe.

For the pastry
8 oz (225 g) plain flour
2 oz (50 g) butter or margarine
2 oz (50 g) lard
Cold water (approximately 4 tbsp)

For the filling
1lb (500 g) beef mince
1 large onion
2 tsp gravy browning
¼ mug of cold water

¼ cup of milk for glazing

Method
1. Make the pastry by sifting the flour into a large mixing bowl then adding the fat to the bowl in small pieces and rubbing the fat and flour together with your fingertips until the mixture resembles medium-fine breadcrumbs.
2. Make a well in the centre of the flour then add about half the given quantity of water and mix together with your hand or a tablespoon to make the dough, adding a little more water if necessary.
3. Turn the dough out onto a floured surface and knead for a minute or two until the dough is smooth and workable, then

wrap in cling film or foil and keep in the fridge while you make the pie filling.

4. Cook the mince in a large pan while you finely chop the onion, then add the onion to the pan and cook for a few more minutes until the mince has browned and the onion is soft.

5. Meanwhile, preheat the oven to Gas Mark 6 (200°C) and use a mug to make six circles on a sheet of greaseproof paper (or one circle for however many pies you're making). Place a greaseproof circle at the base of each hole in the tin and grease the whole of the inside.

6. As soon as the meat is cooked, strain as much of the fatty liquid out of the pan as you can and mix 2 teaspoons of gravy browning in ¼ mug of cold water, making sure there are no lumps.

7. Pour the gravy browning into the pan with the meat and stir well for a minute or two until the sauce thickens, then remove the pan from the heat.

8. Roll out the pastry to about ⅛ in (3 mm) thick; use a side plate or saucer to cut out six pie bottoms, and a mug to make six pie lids, re-rolling the pastry trimmings as necessary.

9. Carefully place one large circle of pastry in each hole in the tin; prick with a fork several times then fill with the meat mixture, leaving about ¼ in (5 mm) of pastry at the top.

10. Brush the pastry edges of the pies with a little milk then put a lid on top of each pie and fold the top edge of the pastry over the lid, pressing down gently to seal the pies.

11. Prick the top of the pies with a fork, brush with more milk and bake the pies in a hot oven for about 25 minutes, or until the pastry is golden.

12. Serve with mashed potatoes and parsley liquor.

How to make liquor

If you don't have fresh chicken stock, use the water you've boiled the potatoes in, or even a mixture of each. And although it's better to use fresh, chopped flat-leaf parsley, dried herbs are more than good enough.

2 oz (50 g) butter or margarine
1 tbsp cornflour
1 pint (500 ml) fresh chicken stock *or* 1 pint (500 ml) potato
    water, or a mixture of stock and water)
1 tbsp vinegar (preferably white wine vinegar, but brown malt will do)
A handful of fresh parsley *or* 2 tbsp dried parsley
Salt & pepper

Method
1. Melt the butter or margarine in a saucepan and stir in the cornflour to make a paste.
2. Gradually pour in the stock or water, plus vinegar, and whisk continuously to prevent lumps forming.
3. Add the finely chopped fresh parsley to the sauce and season with a very little salt and pepper.
4. Serve with the pies and mashed potatoes.

Tip
Instead of using cornflour, thicken a watery sauce with a small cup of (uncooked) couscous stirred in a few minutes before serving.

SWEDISH MEATBALLS & CREAM SAUCE

You can buy both of these in the Ikea food shops (frozen meatballs, packet mix sauce) but if you fancy the food without the mile-long trip round the store and a 30-minute wait at the checkout – and that doesn't include the hassle of finding a parking space and getting out of the car park afterwards – try making these at home instead. (This amount of meat makes between 25–30 meatballs.)

Redcurrant jelly is a good substitute for the fruit jelly you get in the Ikea restaurants, which is loganberry I think.

For the meatballs
½ lb (225 g) pork mince
½ lb (225 g) beef mince
1 tsp garlic or onion salt
¼ tsp cayenne pepper
Black pepper

For the cream sauce
2 big tsp gravy powder
1 tsp cornflour
1 tsp garlic salt
1 tsp sugar
1 tiny tin (7 fl oz/170 g) evaporated milk
¾ pint (450 ml) water (approx)

Method

1. Make the meatballs by squishing the meat and all the seasonings together in a bowl and rolling the mixture into small balls with your hands. (Don't use flour; just wet your hands with water.) To cook: either flash fry the meatballs for a couple

of minutes in enough hot oil to cover them, then finish in the oven, or bake them in the oven from the start at Gas Mark 6 (200°C) for 15–25 minutes – depending on whether or not they were fried first.

2. Meanwhile, make the cream sauce by pouring the evaporated milk into a measuring jug and topping it up to the ³/₄ pint (450 ml) mark with boiling water.

3. Pour the milk/water mixture into a saucepan and bring *almost* to the boil over a low heat.

4. While you're waiting for the milk to boil, mix the gravy powder, cornflour, sugar and garlic salt with a very little cold water (about 1–2 tbsp) to make a smooth paste in a mug or small bowl.

5. As soon as the milk is hot enough (you may notice the beginnings of a crinkly skin on the surface), add a few tablespoons of the hot milk to the paste, making sure it's well mixed, then pour the warm paste slowly back into the pan, whisking or stirring all the time to make a thick, lump-free sauce.

6. Serve the meatballs with chips or rice, with the sauce poured over the meatballs and the fruit jelly on the side.

MACARONI CHEESE

Mustard powder is ideal for this but if you only have a jar of ready-made, whisk a spoonful into the sauce once you've added the milk. (If you don't have macaroni any other pasta shapes will do.)

I find it hard to give precise quantities for a cheese sauce because I never measure the quantities when I make it myself, but you won't go far wrong with these and you can always whisk in a little more milk at the end if you think the sauce is too thick. And although you're supposed to add the grated cheese to the finished sauce I throw the whole lot in with the milk and it works just fine.

Macaroni or pasta shapes
2 oz (50 g) butter or margarine
2 tbsp plain flour
1 oz (25 g) cheese
1 pint (500 ml) milk
1 tsp nutmeg
1 tsp mustard powder
Black pepper

Method
1. Put the macaroni in a saucepan of slightly salted boiling water and simmer steadily for about 15 minutes in the usual way, or according to the instructions on the packet.
2. Melt the butter or margarine in a saucepan over a low heat while you sift the flour, mustard powder and nutmeg together.
3. Stir the flour mixture into the melted fat with a wooden spoon and keep stirring for a couple of minutes until the paste is shiny and slipping away from the bottom of the pan.
4. Add the milk, grated cheese and black pepper and keep beating the sauce to prevent lumps forming – or make it easy on yourself to begin with by using a small hand whisk instead of a wooden spoon.
5. Drain the cooked macaroni and put it in a lightly buttered ovenproof dish then cover with the cheese sauce and pop it in the oven at Gas Mark 7 (220ºC) or under a preheated grill for a couple of minutes until it browns and bubbles.
6. Serve with grilled crispy bacon, grilled tomatoes and spinach.

TOAD IN THE MUSH

Dried packet soup still exists, despite the influx of soups in cartons and pouches in the supermarket chill cabinet. Knorr's English Broccoli and Stilton is perfect for this.

1 packet of instant dried soup
1 small packet of instant mashed potato
Milk
Water
Black pepper
Sausages

Method
1. Cook sausages in the usual way.
2. Make the soup with milk, or a combination of milk and water, according to the instructions on the packet.
3. Take the soup off the heat when cooked and beat in the instant mashed potato straight from the packet until the 'mush' is light and fluffy. Season with black pepper and serve with sausages and green vegetables.

MEAT & POTATO PUDDING

Because you fry the meat before you steam the pudding, the cooking time is about an hour shorter than it would be for a traditional steak and kidney pudding; around 2 hours as opposed to 3 hours plus.

Minced beef is sold in similar sized packs practically everywhere although the weight varies between 400 g–500 g (about 1 lb) from one supermarket to another. A 400 g pack with roughly the same amount of potatoes is perfect for a standard size 1½–2 pint (750 ml–1 litre) pudding basin so if you're using one of the bigger packets of meat reduce the quantity of potatoes accordingly.

For the pastry
½ lb (225 g) self-raising flour
4 oz (100 g) suet
6 fl oz (175 ml) cold water (approx)

For the pudding
Approximately 1 lb (400 g–500 g) minced beef
1 lb (400 g–500 g) potatoes (approx)
1 onion
1 beef stock cube
1 tbsp tomato purée
2 tsp garlic purée
1 tbsp mustard
½ cup of cold water

Method
1. Peel the potatoes; rinse in cold water and cut into large cubes then put the potatoes straight into a saucepan of boiling water and simmer gently for a very few minutes before removing from the heat and rinsing in cold water again.
2. Dry fry the minced beef and add the chopped onion, breaking up the meat occasionally with a wooden spoon. Once the meat has browned, strain as much of the fat out of the pan as you can.
3. Put the beef stock cube, tomato purée, garlic purée, mustard and water into the pan with the meat and cook for a couple more minutes before adding the potatoes and removing the pan from the heat.

4. Make the pastry by sifting the flour into a large mixing bowl with the suet then making a well in the centre and gradually adding the water to make a soft but still fairly stiff dough.

5. Roll the dough out on a floured surface to make a big enough circle to fill the pudding basin, with at least an inch (2.5 cm) overlapping, then cut out one quarter of the pastry circle to make the lid.

6. Line the pudding basin with the large piece of pastry, pressing it down to the bottom of the basin and sealing the join with your fingers.

7. Fill the pudding with the meat mixture, then put the pastry lid on and trim the overlap, leaving just enough to fold inwards over the lid and seal the pudding. (Make it stick by painting a little water along the edge of the pudding with your fingers first.)

8. Cover the pudding with a double layer of greaseproof paper and one layer of foil with a pleat in the middle to allow the pudding to expand.

9. Steam the pudding in a large saucepan with a lid on for about 2 hours, checking the water level in the saucepan every so often to see that it doesn't boil dry.

10. Spoon the pudding straight from the basin, or hold an oven tray firmly over the top and tip the basin upside down so the pudding slides out slowly. Make extra gravy if you think the pudding is too dry and serve with mixed vegetables or baked beans.

Tip
If you have limited cupboard space and don't want to store too much flour, just buy plain and add a couple of teaspoons of baking powder to make self-raising. The ratio is approximate and varies from one source to another, so I use 1 rounded tsp with smaller amounts of flour – less than ½ lb (225 g) – a generous 1½ tsp per ½ lb (225 g) and 2 heaped tsp for larger quantities, including anything up to and slightly above 1 lb (450 g).

SAUSAGES IN ONION GRAVY WITH ROOT VEGETABLE CRUSH

A crush is just a neat culinary term for what you get when you mash the wrong type of potatoes (i.e. it's a bit lumpy), which would also apply to this recipe if the vegetables you use don't cook completely in sync with each other, so call this a root vegetable mash if you get a completely smooth result and a crush if you don't.

This amount of gravy is enough for at least four servings so if you want more, double it. The type and quantity of vegetables is just a guide.

Sausages (any number)
1–2 onions
4 tsp gravy browning
½ pint (300 ml) water
½ glass of sherry or cider
1 turnip
1 parsnip
2 potatoes

Butter
Milk
1 small swede
4 carrots
Oil

Method

1. Warm some oil in a large ovenproof dish with the oven set at Gas Mark 5 (190°C) and peel and slice the onions.
2. Put the sausages in the ovenproof dish and cook for about 15 minutes before you add the onions. (Make sure the onions are well coated with the oil.)
3. Meanwhile, peel and chop the vegetables to roughly the same size, then bring them to the boil in a large saucepan of cold water, cover with a lid and simmer gently for about 15 minutes, or until the vegetables are just soft. Strain; add a lump of butter and a splash of milk to the pan, then mash.
4. Pour ½ pint (250 ml) of boiling water into a measuring jug and mix 4 teaspoons of gravy browning to a paste in a small bowl or cup with a little more cold water.
5. When the sausages are cooked, spoon the onions into a clean saucepan, leaving any excess oil behind, pour in the boiling water and put the pan over a low heat. (Leave the sausages in the oven on a very low heat while you make the gravy.)
6. Add the diluted gravy browning to the pan followed by the sherry or cider, stirring constantly with a fork or a small hand whisk to prevent lumps. Keep stirring for a couple of minutes until the gravy thickens.
7. Put the sausages onto plates, cover with the onion gravy and serve with the vegetables.

KEBABS

A friend of mine who cooks a lot of turkey always refers to the dark meat as poor man's lamb because she swears that's just what it tastes like …

Anyway, I'd normally make kebabs with the remains of a leg of lamb, which we don't have very often, but I've also made kebabs with patties of minced lamb mixed with leftover sausages, which are just as good and probably not all that different from what (I'd like to think) is in the meat mixture you get on the spike in a kebab shop …

But no recipe need ever be completely authentic as long as it tastes good and contains plenty of nutrients, and when you think about it, a kebab with lots of salad – especially in wholemeal pitta bread – is pretty healthy all round, whether you've made it from a cooked turkey drumstick cut into chunks, minced meat patties or lamb from a leftover joint. You don't need much meat either; about 1 lb (550 g) should be enough to make kebabs for at least four people.

For the kebabs
1 lb (500 g) + meat
Wholemeal pitta bread
Iceberg lettuce
Tomatoes
Cucumber
Red onion

For the sauce
2 tbsp natural yoghurt
1 tbsp vinegar

1 tsp mint
1 tsp sugar
½ tsp each: curry powder, turmeric, onion or garlic salt

Method
1. If you've cooked the meat from scratch keep it warm while you prepare the sauce and salad, otherwise thoroughly reheat the previously cooked meat once everything else is ready.
2. Wash, dry and finely shred the lettuce. Slice the tomatoes, cucumber and onion into rings.
3. Make the dressing by mixing all the ingredients together in a small bowl, adding more yoghurt or a spoonful of mayonnaise for a thicker sauce.
4. Warm the pitta bread under a preheated grill for about 2 minutes, turning once, then split them open with a sharp knife as soon as the bread is cool enough to handle.
5. Fill the pittas with the salad and hot meat, adding a spoonful of sauce to each one.

HOME-BAKED BEANS

Why would you bother making baked beans when the tinned variety are so cheap and only take about 30 seconds to warm up in the microwave? Well for a start, home-cooked baked beans are something altogether different, and I'm not suggesting you cook them all the time – or even most of the time – but every now and then it's worth making them yourself simply because they taste good and are at least as cost-effective as tinned beans, especially if you make full use of the oven by cooking a casserole, a pot roast, or some barbecue beans at the same time.

Both bean recipes make good vegetarian pizza toppings as well as being perfect with sausages, burgers, chicken, or even cheese on toast.

This recipe is as basic as it gets but you can also add grated carrots or replace half the quantity of tomato juice with beer for a bit of variety. (Go easy on the black treacle though; if you add more than a couple of tablespoons you can taste the iron over the other flavours, which isn't so good.)

1 lb (500 g) haricot beans (dry weight)
2 onions
2 tbsp black treacle
1 litre carton of tomato juice
1 tbsp English or French mustard
Olive oil

Method
1. Soak the beans in plenty of cold water overnight.
2. Drain the beans, put them in a very large saucepan with enough fresh, cold water to cover and bring to the boil over a high heat. (Cover the saucepan with a lid to speed the process up.)
3. Once the water's boiling, remove the lid, turn the heat down and simmer the beans for 25–30 minutes.
4. Meanwhile, warm some olive oil in another large pan and fry the chopped onions, adding the treacle, mustard and tomato juice as soon as the onions are soft and bringing the liquid to the boil.
5. Drain the beans and put them in a very large ovenproof casserole dish with the onion and tomato mixture, cover with a lid and cook in a low, preheated oven, Gas Mark 2–3 (160–170ºC) for 2–3 hours or until the beans are just soft. (Home-cooked baked beans have a bit more bite than tinned beans so don't expect them to have exactly the same soft, squishy texture.)

> **Tip**
> If you don't have tomato juice, whiz two tins of chopped or plum tomatoes in a blender or food processor: 2 tins make just over 1 pint (approximately 500 ml) of juice.

BARBECUE BEANS

The quantities given here make a lot of beans – at a guess, I'd say about a dozen servings – but they do keep well in the fridge for a few days and can be served alongside, or mixed in with, lots of other dishes – as a baked potato filling, or added to chilli con carne, for instance.

1 lb (500 g) kidney beans (dry weight)
4 tins of chopped tomatoes
1 red onion
4 tbsp cider vinegar
1 tbsp soy sauce
1 tbsp Worcestershire sauce
2 tsp mustard
1 tsp chilli powder

Method
1. Soak the beans in plenty of cold water overnight.
2. Drain the beans and rinse thoroughly, put in a very large saucepan with enough fresh cold water to cover and bring to the boil over a high heat.
3. Boil rapidly for 30 minutes then drain the beans and rinse through with more fresh cold running water.
4. Transfer the beans to a large ovenproof dish and heat the

chopped tomatoes with the chopped onion, vinegar, soy sauce, Worcestershire sauce, mustard and chilli powder; ideally, in the same pan you used to cook the beans.

5. As soon as the sauce boils, pour over the beans, stir well and cover the casserole with a lid or a layer of foil.
6. Cook in a low oven, Gas Mark 2–3 (160–170°C), for about 3 hours, or until the beans are just soft.

SWEET POTATO PASTIES

I first thought of making these when I had a bowl of leftover egg yolks and half a carton of single cream slightly past its best in the fridge.

Mix other bits and pieces into the filling if you like, but these little pasties are nice enough with just the sweet potatoes and seeds.

375 g packet (just under 1 lb) of ready-made puff pastry
2 sweet potatoes (any size)
1 tsp mustard seeds
1 tsp cumin seeds
1 tsp caraway seeds
2–3 egg yolks
Single cream (roughly ½ small carton)
1 tbsp butter
¼ cup of milk
Salt & pepper

Method
1. Take the pastry out of the fridge, remove the outer packaging and leave to stand at room temperature while you peel the

sweet potatoes, bring them to the boil in a saucepan of cold water and simmer gently for about 10 minutes, or until they're just soft.

2. Meanwhile, toast the seeds in a non-stick pan over a gentle heat for a few minutes until you can smell the flavours coming through quite strongly and some of the seeds start to pop.

3. Mash the sweet potatoes with the egg yolks, single cream, butter and seeds and season with salt and pepper.

4. Leave the sweet potato mash to cool while you take the rectangular sheet of pastry out of its wrapping and place it flat on a floured work surface with the long side towards you.

5. Grease two baking sheets and preheat the oven to Gas Mark 6 (200°C).

6. Carefully roll the pastry rectangle into a square shape, starting from the middle and making sure the pastry maintains the same thickness all over.

7. Cut the pastry into four pieces then cut each piece in two so you have eight rectangles. Place the rectangles on the baking sheets and brush the edges with a little milk.

8. Spoon the filling onto one half of each piece of pastry then fold the other half over, seal the edges with a fork and brush the pasties with more milk.

9. Bake in the oven for 20–25 minutes until the pastry is puffed and golden.

SOUP

Soup's a great comfort food. The first two recipes are very British, filling and ideal in winter; the third one is for mums (and dads) who want to cut calories, and the last one is perfect for young children.

CREAM OF TOMATO SOUP (WITHOUT THE CREAM)

This is the cheaper alternative to a regular 'cream of' recipe because it gives soup the same creamy consistency even though it doesn't actually contain any cream. I got this idea from the exceptionally busy mother of one of my daughter's friends, who also happens to be a very good cook, and although she didn't say where it came from, I'd guess it was originally a wartime recipe, firstly because using basic store cupboard ingredients in place of expensive, hard-to-get-hold-of foods was a favourite trick in those days and, secondly, because it sounds exactly like something my most thrifty grandmother would have made – and she used to mash odd bits of soap together and make new lipsticks by melting down old ones …

1 sweet potato
6 carrots
1 large onion
1 clove of garlic
2 tins chopped tomatoes
2 pints (1 litre) chicken stock
1 oz (25 g) butter or margarine (approx)
1 heaped tbsp flour
Salt & pepper
Oil

Method

1. Peel and chop the sweet potato, carrots, onion and garlic; warm a little oil in a very large saucepan and gently fry the vegetables for a few minutes until the onion is soft.
2. Add the chopped tomatoes to the pan and stir well.
3. Meanwhile, melt the butter in a separate (much smaller) saucepan and stir in the flour, mixing well to make a smooth paste; cook it out for a minute.
4. Pour about ½ pint (250 ml or 1 mugful) of the chicken stock into the pan with the paste and stir or whisk quickly and continuously for a minute or two to make a smooth sauce.
5. Add the sauce to the vegetables in the pan and mix well, followed by the remaining 1½ pints (850 ml) of chicken stock, stirring well again.
6. Bring to the boil then turn the heat right down, cover with a lid and simmer gently for about half an hour.
7. Allow the soup to cool then blend in a liquidizer or food processor and season with salt and pepper.

Tip
Wash out empty plastic milk bottles and use them for freezing home-made stock, soups and sauces. Unlike food bags, they hold their shape and are easier to stack neatly, and this is a good way of knowing how much stock you've got according to the size of the bottle it's stored in.

ROASTED PARSNIP SOUP

The parsnips aren't actually roasted; they're shallow fried to a deep golden brown on the hob, which gives them the same colour and flavour as parsnips baked in the oven. As usual, quantities don't have to be precise, so buy any largish pre-packed bag of parsnips or a couple of pounds (about 1 kg) of loose ones.

Parsnips are especially cheap around Christmas until the end of January when they're in season.

1 bag of parsnips
1 onion
½ bulb of fennel
2 cloves of garlic
Maple syrup
1 rounded tsp ginger
½ tsp nutmeg
1 lemon
Lemon juice
1 pint (500 ml) chicken stock
½ pint (250 ml) milk
Salt & pepper
Margarine
Instant mashed potato

Method
1. Roughly chop the onion and fennel, including the green leafy bit at the top; peel and chop the parsnips into chunks and cut the lemon into quarters, removing the pips and pithy bit in the centre.
2. Melt some margarine in a large saucepan – you could use butter but because the soup is quite rich you may as well use a lighter fat – and add the parsnips, onion, fennel, crushed garlic, lemon

quarters, nutmeg, ginger and a good squeeze of maple syrup. (Give the lemon pieces a little squeeze as you put them in.)

3. Fry the vegetables on high for about 10 minutes until the parsnips are golden and 'roasted'.
4. Pour on the chicken stock and milk, stirring well, bring to the boil and simmer for about half an hour.
5. Allow the soup to cool just a little, then remove the lemon quarters, whisk in some instant mashed potato to get the consistency you want (while the soup is still warm), then blend in a liquidizer or food processor.
6. Adjust the consistency of the soup if necessary with a little more instant mash and season with salt, pepper and more lemon juice.

Tip
Instant mashed potato is a great thickener for soups, stews and some sauces.

MIXED VEGETABLE SKINNY SOUP

This soup is very similar to the one in the Cabbage Soup Diet, except that it contains considerably more flavour than the original, you're allowed to fry the vegetables first, instead of just boiling them, and apparently it still helps you lose weight even though you don't have to eat it for breakfast, lunch and dinner to the exclusion of everything else.

Even so, on its own this soup is still about as basic and boring as it gets and although it keeps in the fridge for a day or two it doesn't freeze well. (It's also greatly improved if you top the finished soup with broken up cream crackers covered in Marmite.)

Use any kind of stock you like, but fresh chicken stock or a mixture of ready-made and fresh stock is best.

1 Savoy cabbage
1 small bunch of spring onions
1 head of celery
2 large peppers, any colour
Carrots
Mushrooms
2 cloves of garlic
2 tins chopped tomatoes
4 pints (2 litres) stock
2 heaped tsp 5 Spice
2 tsp ginger
Soy sauce
Sesame oil
Salt & pepper

Method

1. Wash, peel and finely chop the spring onions, celery, peppers, carrots and mushrooms, and finely shred the cabbage.
2. Warm some sesame oil in a very large pan; fry the onions, celery and peppers with the spices until the onion softens then add the crushed garlic and the rest of the vegetables including the chopped tomatoes and give it a good stir.
3. Pour in the stock and a generous amount of soy sauce then stir again, turn the heat down, cover with a lid and allow the soup to simmer gently for about half an hour.
4. Don't blend the finished soup. Season with salt and pepper and serve with crackers and Marmite (see above).

PASTA SOUP

You can add cooked pasta to any soup, of course, but with this one you actually cook the pasta in the soup, so it's doubly easy to do on a busy school night when you want to get the children fed and off to bed as quickly and painlessly as possible.

Pasta shapes
1 tin of baked beans
2 tins of tomatoes
1 onion
1 pint (500 ml) stock
Tomato purée
Garlic purée
Herbes de Provence
Salt & pepper

Method
1. Roughly chop the onion then put in a food processor or blender with the baked beans and tinned tomatoes and whiz for a minute or so until smooth.
2. Pour a pint (500 ml) of (any) stock into a very large saucepan and mix with the puréed beans, tomatoes, onion, herbs and a little tomato and garlic purée.
3. Bring to the boil over a medium heat and when the soup is bubbling add the pasta and simmer for about 20 minutes, stirring frequently until the pasta is just cooked.
4. Adjust the seasoning with salt and pepper or a little more tomato purée if necessary and serve with grated cheese.

Tip
Never throw out surplus cooked rice, pasta, couscous or quinoa, which can be added to soups and salads.

POT ROASTS

A pot roast is a wonderful thing for a number of reasons. For a start, the preparation time is very, very short – 15 minutes or thereabouts – the ingredients are basic and affordable, you can guarantee a good result with the cheapest cuts of meat, and once you've got it into the oven it just takes care of itself. Simply add potatoes (or not) and some extra, super-quick vegetables from the freezer and you're done.

Pot roasts also keep for at least two or three days in the fridge and freeze well, so if you want to make one in advance you can either cook it for 2 hours to begin with (depending on the size and weight of the meat) and reheat for another hour or so at the same temperature later on, or cook it completely the first time and reheat it in the microwave when you want to eat it.

If cooking a previously frozen pot roast, allow it to defrost thoroughly then reheat it slowly in a low oven, Gas Mark 2–3 (160–170ºC), making doubly sure the food is piping hot all the way through.

Of course, you can just as easily use beef topside or a leg of lamb for a pot roast, but if you can get the same result with a more cost-effective cut of meat and you want to save money, what's the point? Pork shoulder or knuckle are ideal, as is belly of pork, although it's a bit fattier; also beef brisket and lamb neck fillet are good.

Finally, producing the perfect pot roast – and really there's no other kind – can make anyone appear as super-efficient and creative in the kitchen as Bree Van de Kamp, whether you are in fact a true domestic goddess, or just an average desperate housewife.

PORK AND CRANBERRY POT ROAST

As soon as fresh cranberries appear in the shops in December I buy them two or three bags at a time and use some/freeze some until they disappear straight after Christmas, so the cranberries in this recipe will have already been stewed and sweetened into a kind of purée. (See Deep-Fried Camembert with Cranberry Sauce in Chapter 4, 'For Starters, mains and just desserts'.) You can either make the cranberry purée first or use them straight from the packet, adding a couple of extra tablespoons of sugar (and maybe a spoonful of honey or golden syrup) to the sauce with the tomatoes at Stage 5.

Serves 4
1 small shoulder of pork
Carrots
Baby onions
2 cloves of garlic
1 tin of chopped tomatoes
Tomato purée
Cranberry purée *or* 1 packet (approx 300 g/½ lb+) of fresh
    cranberries
1 tbsp sugar
Oil

Method
1. Preheat the oven to Gas Mark 2–3 (160–170ºC); scrape the carrots and chop into large chunks, peel the baby onions and if they're not quite small enough, cut them in half.
2. Warm some oil in a large pan and fry the carrots, onions and garlic for a few minutes over a very high heat until the onions are slightly softer and just beginning to brown.

3. Transfer the vegetables to a very large casserole dish with a slotted spoon then add a little more oil to the pan and stir in the sugar.

4. Put the pork shoulder into the pan and seal the meat using a large spoon and fork to turn the joint over so it browns quickly on all sides, then put the pork in the casserole dish with the vegetables.

5. Add the chopped tomatoes, tomato purée and cranberries (with extra sugar if necessary) to the pan, stirring well to incorporate any residue from the meat into the sauce.

6. Pour the sauce over and around the meat and vegetables in the casserole dish, cover with a lid and cook in the middle of the oven for a minimum 2½–3 hours until the meat is completely tender.

Tip
Some fruits work well in pot roasts – dried or tinned apricots and prunes, apples, or fruit purées (see Pork and Cranberry Pot Roast above) – because they add flavour and the acid in the fruit helps to tenderize the meat.

BEEF & POTATO POT ROAST

As a rough guide, do as many carrots and onions as you think you'd need to feed, say, six people.

1½–2 lb (750 g–1 kg) beef brisket
Carrots
Baby onions
1 turnip

4 largish potatoes
1½ pints (850 ml) beef stock (1 stock cube)
½ glass of sherry
1 big tsp of mustard
1 tbsp tomato purée
1 tbsp garlic purée
Oil
Seasoning

Method

1. Preheat the oven to Gas Mark 2–3 (160–170ºC); warm some oil in a large deep-sided pan while you scrape the carrots, peel the onions and turnip and chop all the vegetables into large chunks.
2. Cook the vegetables over a high heat for a few minutes until the onions are softer and slightly golden then transfer to a very large casserole dish.
3. Meanwhile, peel and cut the potatoes into rounds.
4. Season the beef then put it into the pan and seal the meat, using a large spoon and fork to turn the joint over so it browns quickly on all sides.
5. Put the beef in the casserole dish with the vegetables then add the beef stock, sherry, mustard, tomato and garlic purées to the pan, stir well and bring to the boil.
6. Pour the liquid over the beef and vegetables in the casserole dish then cover the surface of the casserole with slices of potato.
7. Cover the casserole with a lid and cook in the oven for between 2–2½ hours.
8. Take the lid off, turn the oven up to Gas Mark 6 (200ºC) and cook for another 20 minutes until the potato slices on the surface are crisp and brown.

> **Tip**
> Add herbs and spices to pot roasts according to taste, also bouquet garni bags, bay leaves, or cloves pressed into baby onions and removed after cooking.

CHICKEN & ROSEMARY IN WHITE WINE STOCK

A large chicken cooked in half a bottle of wine isn't as economical as a pot roast made with a cheaper cut of meat in plain stock, but still …

Although I nearly always use dried herbs and spices, fresh rosemary is perfect for this. (It's about the only edible thing I have growing outside in the garden at the moment so I do tend to use it all the time.)

One of those very large, oval casserole dishes with a domed lid is ideal for pot roasting chickens, but if you haven't got one and your chicken is too big to put a lid on, just cover the casserole completely in foil.

1 chicken (any size)
Carrots
Celery
Onions
2 or 3 sprigs of fresh rosemary
½ bottle white wine
½ pint (250 ml) chicken or vegetable stock
A little butter or olive oil
Salt & pepper
Instant gravy granules

Method

1. Preheat the oven to Gas Mark 2–3 (160–170ºC).
2. Wash, peel and chop the onions, carrots and celery whichever way you like.
3. Put the chicken in the casserole dish; rub a little butter or olive oil over the skin, season with salt and pepper and surround the chicken with the chopped vegetables and rosemary.
4. Make ½ pint (250 ml) of chicken or vegetable stock with one stock cube and pour the stock and wine into the casserole.
5. Cover with a lid or a tight layer of foil and cook in the oven for about 3 hours; check if the chicken is cooked by sticking a sharp knife or skewer into the leg to see if the juices are running clear.
6. When the chicken is carved up and the rest of the meal is ready, make gravy with the white wine stock; the easiest way is to gradually add the stock to instant gravy granules until you get the consistency you want.

Tip
As long as you seal the meat first you can't really overcook a pot roast as long as it's in a really low oven; approximately Gas Mark 2 (150–160ºC) is ideal. That last half hour is the one that makes all the difference between the meat being simply 'done' and perfectly tender, so don't be afraid to leave it in the oven for a good 3½ or even 4 hours.

CURRY

There's nothing here to rival anything on the menu in your favourite Indian restaurant, but these Brit-friendly curry recipes are perfect if you want to make something spicy and (almost) authentic that won't tie you up in knots even if you're an absolute beginner, or take too long to cook.

Although I sometimes use fresh chillies I tend to rely on ground spices and dried herbs in my everyday cooking, so unless you're really serious about learning how to make classic Indian food, the following ten ingredients are probably all you'll ever need to make a pretty good everyday curry.

Allspice
Chilli powder
Coriander
Cumin
Curry powder (medium)
Garam Masala
Garlic salt
Ginger
Mustard seeds
Turmeric

"Without the curry, boiled rice can be very dull."

C. Northcote Parkinson

CHICKEN TIKKA MASALA

A few years ago Chicken Tikka Masala was voted Britain's national dish, which is a shame in some ways … but never mind, here it is.

This is the home-made version though, so don't expect it to look exactly like the shocking pink Chicken Tikka Masala you find in some Indian restaurants (how do they do that?) but still it's a good one – and much better than some I've come across, I have to say.

This amount of curry sauce would be enough for double the amount of chicken given here; you could also cook the chicken pieces whole if you're making the curry with four fillets, in which case you should make a few cuts in the surface of each fillet with a sharp knife.

2 chicken breast fillets, skin removed
1 onion
2 cloves of garlic
¼ tsp turmeric
½–1 tsp cayenne pepper
1 tsp cumin
1 tsp coriander
1 tsp cinnamon
1 tsp allspice
2 tsp paprika
1 tin chopped tomatoes
2 tbsp tomato purée
3 tbsp natural yoghurt
Oil
Butter

Method

1. Wash and cut the chicken into large chunks.
2. Finely chop the onion and crush or finely chop the garlic.
3. Melt some butter and oil in a large pan; fry the onion and garlic until soft and slightly golden then add the spices, stir well, and cook for a couple of minutes.
4. Stir in the chopped tomatoes and tomato purée; add the chicken, making sure the meat is covered by the sauce, then cover with a lid and simmer very gently for 20–25 minutes, depending on the size of the chicken pieces.
5. Add the yoghurt to the pan and warm through for another 5–10 minutes.
6. Serve with rice and sprinkle the curry with chopped coriander leaves (or even fresh) if you have them.

LAMB KEEMA

This comes out mild to medium spicy – at least that's how it seems to me. If you make curries a lot you'll know how much or how little you need to use of each of the spices on the list; as usual this is just a rough guide.

1 lb (500 g) lamb mince
1 onion
2 cloves of garlic
1 tsp hot curry powder
1tsp ginger
1tsp coriander
½ tsp turmeric
2 tsp cumin
2 tsp sugar

2 tsp mint

Lime juice

1 tin chopped tomatoes

1 tin garden peas

Method

1. Fry the lamb mince in a large pan over a high heat, breaking up the meat with a wooden spoon.

2. Meanwhile, add the chopped onion and garlic to the pan and cook for a few minutes until the meat has browned through and the onion is soft.

3. Strain as much fatty liquid out of the pan as you can and add the spices, sugar, mint, lime juice and chopped tomatoes.

4. Stir well, cover with a lid and simmer gently for about 30 minutes.

5. Add the tinned peas to the pan and cook for another 10 minutes.

6. Serve with rice or couscous.

CARIBBEAN-STYLE CHICKEN CURRY

This dish works very well with cheaper cuts of chicken on the bone – thighs, drumsticks or breast – which can often be found in large mixed packets of roughly eight pieces (including free-range) in the supermarket.

Chicken x 2 packets of mixed pieces on the bone

1 onion

3 spring onions

1 clove of garlic

1 red chilli

1 small red pepper
1 small green pepper
2 tsp chicken seasoning
1 tsp each of: chilli powder, coriander, allspice, celery salt and garlic
   salt
1 tbsp tomato purée
1 x 200 ml carton of pineapple juice
Oil
Butter

Method

1. Remove the chicken skin and put all chicken pieces in a large non-metallic dish.
2. Mix the chicken seasoning and the rest of the spices together in a small bowl then coat the chicken pieces and leave covered in the fridge for at least half an hour, and preferably overnight.
3. Heat plenty of oil in a large, deep-sided pan and quickly fry the chicken pieces a few at a time until brown on all sides, keeping the cooked meat warm at the bottom of a very low oven.
4. When all the chicken is cooked, fry the onions, spring onions, crushed garlic, chilli and chopped peppers in the remainder of the oil then add the pineapple juice and tomato purée to the pan and stir well.
5. Put the chicken pieces back in the pan, stir again then cover and simmer gently for 15–20 minutes until the chicken is cooked through and the liquid is reduced.
6. Serve with plain boiled rice.

GREEN BANANA CURRY

Green bananas – not to be confused with regular unripe bananas or plantain, which is also green and looks like a very large banana – are small, green and stumpy with blackish patches when they're ready to eat. Like plantain, green bananas are easier to pare with a sharp knife rather than peel, and like regular bananas they soon soften up when cooked, although they taste (I think) quite a lot like potatoes. Confused? You won't be – assuming you don't know everything there is to know about green bananas already, in which case this recipe for green banana curry may be a bit too basic for you, and probably isn't even authentic either.

Serve with some sort of meat curry and rice, or just with rice as a vegetarian main course.

2–2½ lb (1 kg +) green bananas
1 bunch of spring onions
2 green chillies
2 tsp curry powder
2 tsp cinnamon
1 tsp chilli powder
½ tsp turmeric
2 tins of coconut milk
½ mug of couscous
Lemon juice
Lime juice
Oil

Method
1. Mix the curry powder, cinnamon, chilli powder and turmeric together in a bowl.

2. Remove banana skins with a sharp knife, cut into chunks and coat with the spices.
3. Top and tail the spring onions and cut them lengthways; deseed and finely chop the chillies.
4. Warm some oil in a large pan and fry the green bananas, spring onions and chillies together for a couple of minutes until the bananas are browning nicely and the onions have softened.
5. Add the coconut milk to the pan and bring to the boil then turn the heat right down and simmer gently for 10–15 minutes until the bananas feel 'done' when you pierce them with a sharp knife.
6. Turn the heat off and add the couscous to the curry; sprinkle (or squeeze) some lemon and lime juice into the pan according to taste then stir well and leave for about 10 minutes so the couscous cooks gently in the sauce. Serve with rice.

MEATBALL CURRY

Half the amount of onion, garlic and spices goes into the meatballs, the other half into the sauce; this recipe is as simple and straightforward as it gets. (And I don't see why it couldn't work equally well with pork or beef mince.) You can fry the meatballs if you prefer, but it's much easier and less messy to put them on a lightly greased baking tray and cook them in the oven.

Serves 4 (makes at least 24 meatballs)
1lb (450–500 g) lamb mince
2 onions
2 cloves of garlic
1 egg
1 tin of coconut milk

Oil

Butter

2 tsp chilli powder

2 tsp curry powder or fenugreek

2 tsp allspice

2 tsp cumin

2 tsp turmeric

2 tsp ginger

½ cup couscous

Method

1. Preheat the oven to Gas Mark 6 (200ºC) and grease a baking tray or Pyrex dish.

2. Put the lamb mince in a large bowl with 1 finely chopped onion, 1 clove of crushed garlic and 1 teaspoon each of chilli powder, curry powder (or fenugreek), allspice, cumin, turmeric and ginger, plus the egg, and squish it all together with your hands.

3. Roll the meat mixture into balls (don't use flour, it works better without), putting them straight onto the greased tray. Bake the meatballs in the oven for 20–25 minutes and shake them up on the tray at least once during cooking time.

4. Meanwhile, warm some butter and oil in a large saucepan and fry the second finely chopped onion and clove of garlic until soft, then add another teaspoon each of chilli powder, curry powder (or fenugreek), allspice, cumin, turmeric and ginger and cook for a few more minutes.

5. Empty the tin of coconut milk into a large measuring jug, make up to 1 pint (500 ml) with cold water and add to the onion and spices in the pan. (If you haven't got a measuring jug add the coconut milk then half fill the empty tin with cold water and add that to the pan.)

6. Bring the sauce to the boil, stirring frequently, and allow to simmer for a good 10 minutes to reduce the amount of liquid by about a third.
7. Turn the heat right down, add the cooked meatballs and simmer gently for about 30 minutes. If the sauce is still thinner than you'd like it to be, stir a small cup of couscous into the curry, allowing another 5–10 minutes for the couscous to swell and soften, before serving.
8. Serve with plain boiled rice.

CREAMY VEGETABLE CURRY

Good as a side dish with a dry meat curry and rice, or as a main dish for vegetarians. As a rough guide, the ratio of cauliflower to carrots to green beans should be about 4:2:1.

1 large cauliflower
Carrots
Green beans
½ large carton of natural yoghurt
½ tin of coconut milk
3 big tbsp gram flour
1 mug of cold water
1 big tsp each of: chilli powder, curry powder, coriander, coriander leaf, mustard seeds
2 tsp cumin seeds
2 tsp salt
Oil

Method

1. Prepare the vegetables and cut into approximately same-size pieces then put the carrots in cold water and bring to the boil, adding the cauliflower and green beans about halfway through the carrots' cooking time.

2. Meanwhile, sift the flour, salt and spices (not the seeds) into a bowl, add the yoghurt, coconut milk and water and whisk with a fork till smooth.

3. Warm some oil in a large pan and fry the mustard seeds for a minute then add the cumin seeds and fry for another minute.

4. Strain the vegetables as soon as they're cooked and set aside while you add the sauce to the pan with the seeds and bring it to the boil, stirring all the time.

5. Simmer the sauce for a couple of minutes then adjust the seasoning, add the vegetables to the pan and warm through.

QUICK CURRIED PRAWNS

If you're using frozen prawns, defrost them first according to the instructions on the packet, or more quickly by rinsing them in a colander under the cold tap, leaving them to stand for about 15 minutes then rinsing thoroughly again.

1 large packet of prawns
4 sticks of celery
1 red pepper
1 green pepper
1 onion
1 cooking apple
Sultanas
½ glass of white wine

¼ pint (150 ml) stock
2 tbsp tomato purée
2 tbsp natural yoghurt
Worcestershire sauce
1 tbsp curry powder
½ tbsp cumin
1 tsp ginger
1 tbsp plain or gram flour
Lemon juice
Oil
Salt & pepper

Method
1. Warm some oil in a large pan while you peel and chop the celery, peppers and onion.
2. Fry the vegetables and spices over a medium heat while you peel and dice the apple then add the apple to the pan with the (defrosted) prawns and a handful of sultanas.
3. Sift the flour into the pan, stir well and cook for another minute.
4. Add the stock, white wine, tomato purée, Worcestershire sauce and lemon juice (both according to taste) to the pan, still stirring, and season with salt and pepper.
5. Cover with a lid and simmer for about 10 minutes until the sauce has thickened and the food is hot.
6. Adjust the seasoning, stir in the yoghurt and serve with couscous or plain boiled rice.

RICE & LENTILS

I have to admit I really only enjoy vegetarian food if I can have a bit of meat with it, but this recipe is completely perfect in its own right, so you don't have to try and improve it by adding sausages, chicken or pork chops unless you really want to ...

6 oz (150 g) basmati rice
6 oz (150 g) brown or green lentils or yellow split peas
2 onions
Mushrooms
3/4 tsp cumin seeds
3/4 tsp turmeric
3/4 tsp cinnamon
2 tsp sugar
Olive oil
Vegetable oil
1 1/4 pints (approx 750 ml) water
2 eggs
Tomatoes
Cucumber
Salt & pepper

Method
1. Soak the lentils in cold water overnight. Rinse the soaked lentils or yellow split peas thoroughly then put them in a pan with approximately 1 1/4 pints (750 ml) of cold water, bring to the boil and simmer gently for about 25 minutes until the lentils are soft. (Don't strain the water away.)
2. Warm a very large pan on the hob and toast the cumin seeds for a minute until you start to smell the flavour coming off

them (don't let them burn) then add some olive oil to the pan followed by the cinnamon, turmeric and rice.

3. Stir well and make sure the rice is coated with the oil and spices.
4. Add the cooked lentils and their water to the pan with the rice, season with salt and pepper, bring to the boil, cover and simmer very gently over a low heat for about 20 minutes or until the rice is done.
5. Meanwhile, put the eggs into the pan to cook with the rice for 10 minutes then remove with a slotted spoon and set aside.
6. While you're waiting for the rice to cook warm some vegetable oil in a small pan then stir in the sugar. As soon as the oil is darker in colour, add the onions and cook for a few minutes until they're golden, or just the way you like them, then add the mushrooms and cook for another couple of minutes.
7. As soon as the rice is cooked take the pan off the heat and if you think there's still a little too much liquid strain some away.
8. Mix the onions and mushrooms with the rice and lentils and garnish with the chopped hard-boiled eggs, sliced tomatoes and cucumber.

VEGETABLE SAMOSAS

It's hard to say how many samosas you can expect to make with one packet of filo pastry; it depends on the size and how much pastry you waste in the process, but as a rough guide you should get between eight and 12.

There's no need to be nervous about cooking with filo pastry either; it's more resilient than it looks, but for some reason I always find the ready-made filo pastry from the chill cabinet easier to handle than the frozen stuff, I don't know why.

This is yet another good way of using up leftover potatoes – boiled or mashed – although it's easy enough to cook a few potatoes from scratch if you don't have leftovers, and this is one recipe where it won't matter if you resort to a packet of instant mash instead of using fresh potatoes; the overall texture and flavour of the other ingredients is a great disguise. In fact, the best thing would be to mix the potatoes and vegetables with a couple of spoonfuls of ready-made curry paste, but because one of my children is severely allergic to nuts I can't use them – unfortunately, because some of them are really good – which is the only reason this recipe has the spices in powdered form.

Finally, I don't know why anyone would deep-fry samosas when you get a much better result and a lot less grease by simply brushing them with melted butter and baking them in the oven for about ten minutes.

1 packet of filo pastry sheets (^{1}/$_2$ lb/250 g)
^{1}/$_2$ small packet of frozen mixed mini vegetables
2–3 medium-sized potatoes, mashed or boiled
1 tbsp curry powder
1 tbsp cumin
2 oz (50 g) butter
Oil

Method
1. Put the frozen vegetables in a saucepan of boiling water and leave to stand for a couple of minutes while you get the rest of the ingredients ready. (No need to cook them properly, they just need to be softened up a bit.)
2. Drain the vegetables and mix with the mashed potato or diced boiled potatoes and spices.
3. Grease one or two oven trays with oil, preheat the oven to Gas Mark 5 (190ºC) and melt the butter in the microwave.

4. Lay the sheets of filo pastry out on a clean work surface, two or three at a time depending on how much room you've got, and cut into long rectangular strips; you should get about four strips from each sheet of filo.

5. Place a dessertspoonful of filling on the left-hand side of each strip then fold the right-hand side of the pastry over diagonally to make a triangle. Carry on folding the samosa over, keeping the triangular shape, until you come to the end of the pastry, then brush generously with melted butter, gently sealing the joins, and place the samosa on the oven tray.

6. Cook the samosas in the oven for about 10 minutes, or until the pastry is a deep golden brown. Eat hot or cold, with or without rice, or as a side dish with another curry.

SIMPLE NAAN BREAD

There are several ways of making naan bread. This method doesn't use yeast so don't expect the dough to rise anywhere near as dramatically as it otherwise would, but it's still worth spending 10 minutes kneading the first time round for a smooth, springy dough and a fine end result.

If you want to make the bread in advance, brush the rolled out naans with melted butter, layer with cling film and keep in the fridge until you're almost ready to eat them. The ingredients below are enough to make 3–6 naans, depending on size (see step 4).

$^{1}/_{2}$ lb+ (250 g) plain flour
$^{1}/_{2}$ tsp baking powder
2 tsp sugar
$^{1}/_{2}$ tsp salt

$^1/_2$ mug of milk (approx 120 ml)
2 tbsp vegetable oil
Melted butter (approx 1 oz/25 g)

Method
1. Sift the flour, baking powder, sugar and salt together in a large mixing bowl, make a well in the centre and pour in the milk and vegetable oil.
2. Gradually mix the dried ingredients into the liquid to make a soft dough, working from the outside of the bowl inwards and sifting in a little more flour if the dough is too sticky.
3. Turn the dough out onto a floured surface and knead well for about 10 minutes. When the dough is soft, smooth, and feels right, put it into a lightly oiled bowl, cover with a damp cloth and leave in a warm place to prove for at least an hour until the dough has obviously increased in size.
4. Knock back the proved dough – punch it down and knead it thoroughly for a few more minutes in other words – then divide into however many pieces you want and roll each piece out individually into an oval or teardrop shape. Keep each piece of dough at least $^1/_8$ in (3 mm) thick. If you roll them out too thinly the bread will be hard and crisp as opposed to soft and doughy, so if you want five or six naans, make them on the small side.
5. Meanwhile, heat the grill on high and warm a large baking sheet underneath the grill while you melt the butter in the microwave.
6. Brush each naan lightly with the melted butter and put under the grill for a minute or two, until the bread bubbles and browns. (It's as quick as making toast so don't go away and do something else.)

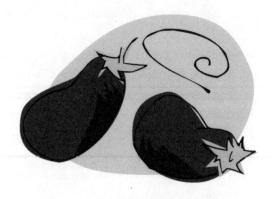

"With packaging materials in short supply people may have to eat fresh food."

The Economist

COOL DINNERS

Cold food really comes into its own in the summer months, whether you want a simple salad with the right dressing or something more substantial, like a simple salad with a large helping of cold meat, pâté, pie, quiche or Scotch eggs …(See also the Raised Pork Pie recipe on page 21 in 'Classics'.)

ASPARAGUS QUICHE

You can buy frozen asparagus or imported fresh asparagus in the supermarket all year round, but fresh is infinitely nicer, I think, especially home-grown asparagus, which is in season from early June until the end of July.

You only want the pretty part of the asparagus for this recipe so use the stalks to make stock or a sauce for a fish dish (see Chapter 3, under 'Leftovers').

Lots of cheeses make good quiches – Cheddar, Caerphilly, Red Leicester, Gruyère – but in this recipe I'd use Cheshire for its lovely mild flavour, or maybe a mixture of Cheshire and one of the others.

The quantities below are enough to fill an 8 in (20 cm) sandwich tin or flan dish.

6 oz (150 g) plain flour
3 oz (75 g) butter or margarine (or 1$\frac{1}{2}$ oz/40 g each of butter and lard)
Approximately 4 tbsp cold water
1 bundle of fresh asparagus
$\frac{1}{2}$ small bundle of spring onions

3 large eggs (or 3 medium eggs + 1 egg yolk)
$^1/_2$ pint (250 ml) single cream
A splash of milk
4 oz (100 g) grated cheese
Salt & pepper

Method
1. Sift the flour into a very large mixing bowl and rub in the fat in small pieces until the mixture resembles medium-fine breadcrumbs.
2. Make a well in the centre then add the cold water and mix it all together, either with your hands or an ordinary knife or a tablespoon, to make a firm, smooth dough.
3. Ideally, wrap the dough in foil or cling film and chill in the fridge for half an hour before turning the dough onto a floured surface and rolling it out to fit the lightly greased tin or flan dish. (If you're short of time you can roll the pastry out straight away; chilling just makes it a bit easier to handle.)
4. Prick the pastry with a fork several times and bake it 'blind' (so the filling can be added when the pastry is cold) by covering the bottom of the flan with a circle of greaseproof paper then weighing the paper down with a handful of dried beans, lentils or rice.
5. Bake in the oven at Gas Mark 4 (180ºC) for 10–15 minutes until the pastry is just golden then remove the dried beans and greaseproof paper.
6. Prepare the asparagus by trimming the tips to about $2^1/_2$ in (5 cm) and putting them in a pan of boiling water (turn the heat off under the pan first) for about 5 minutes before draining.
7. Prepare the spring onions by topping and tailing then cutting them in half, then lengthways into strips so they're roughly the same size as the pieces of asparagus.

8. Beat the eggs, cream, milk and grated cheese together, season with salt and pepper then pour the mixture into the pastry case.
9. Add the asparagus and spring onions to the flan and bake on Gas Mark 4 (180°C) for 30–40 minutes until the pastry is golden brown and the filling is obviously set.
10. Allow the cooked quiche to cool for about half an hour then refrigerate, or serve warm.

MIXED BEAN SALAD

This is best made with a mixture of fresh and tinned beans. Add a finely chopped red onion or a couple of spring onions halved and cut into strips for variation, and swap around the type of beans you use according to what you fancy at the time.

It doesn't matter what kind of dressing you use either – vinaigrette, Thousand Island, or balsamic vinegar straight from the bottle – but, as with most other salads, this one tastes better with than without. (For some ideas for salad dressings see Classic Salads, this chapter.)

1 tin of kidney beans
1 tin of cannellini beans
1 tin of borlotti beans
Green beans
Cherry tomatoes
$^1/_2$ cucumber
1 or 2 peppers (red, yellow, orange or green)
Mixed herbs

Method

1. Trim the green beans at both ends and cook in a saucepan of boiling water, simmering for about 3 minutes once the water starts to bubble. Strain the beans and run them straight under cold water, leaving them to drain for a few minutes before you put them in a large salad bowl.
2. Drain the tins of beans and rinse well in a sieve or colander then add them to the bowl.
3. Wash and halve the cherry tomatoes, wash and cut the cucumber and peppers into chunks, making sure you remove all the seeds from the peppers. (Peel the cucumber if you prefer but there's really no need unless you don't like the skin.)
4. Add everything else to the bowl, sprinkle with herbs, mix well, pour over the salad dressing and store in the fridge for up to 2 days.

CORONATION CHICKEN (OR QUORN)

There are lots of variations of this classic, and the easiest version of all is made by simply mixing a jar of mild curry paste with a carton (or two) of natural yoghurt and adding a handful of sultanas or chopped dried apricots.

My version is not much more complicated than that really, except I don't use ready-made curry paste, and this method works best if you use a food processor to blend the sauce at step 4.

This is a great way to use up leftover chicken; the amount of sauce here is enough for roughly 1lb (450 g) of meat, or a 300 g packet of Quorn.

Chicken (or Quorn)
1 tin of apricots
1 onion
Lemon juice (say 2 tbsp)
3 heaped tbsp of couscous
1 tbsp tomato purée
$^1/_2$ glass white wine
1 level tsp turmeric
1 rounded tsp mild or medium curry powder
1 small sachet of coconut (or $^1/_2$ tin of coconut milk)
2 tbsp natural yoghurt
Butter

Method

1. Warm some butter in a pan and gently fry the chopped onion for a couple of minutes until soft but without any colour.
2. Add the turmeric, curry powder, tomato purée, wine, lemon juice, couscous and all the juice from the tin of apricots to the pan, simmering over a medium-high heat for a few minutes to slightly reduce the liquid.
3. Take the pan off the heat and allow the sauce to cool for about 30 minutes.
4. Whiz the sauce in a food processor with the apricots then add the coconut and yoghurt and blend for another minute.
5. Combine the sauce with the cooked meat or Quorn and store in the fridge.

SCOTCH EGGS

Along with home-made sausage rolls, pizza, chicken nuggets and chips and curry sauce, I'd put Scotch eggs in the healthy junk food category, and once you've made your own you'll never want to eat a bright orange sawdust-and-sausagemeat shop-bought one ever again. (Now that really is junk food.)

Deep-fry them for speed if you like, but you'll get a better result by shallow frying the Scotch eggs for a few minutes, turning them often, then finishing them off in the oven.

Delicious hot or cold.

6 hard-boiled eggs
1 lb (450–500 g) pork mince
1 packet of stuffing mix (any flavour)
Breadcrumbs
Flour
Oil

Method
1. Preheat the oven to Gas Mark 6 (200°C) and warm about ½ in (1.25 cm) of oil in a large pan.
2. Peel the hard-boiled eggs and carefully rinse away any bits of shell and skin before coating them with a little flour.
3. Make up the stuffing mix according to the packet instructions and squish together with the meat.
4. Spread the breadcrumbs out on a dinner plate and divide the meat mixture into 6 pieces; one for each egg.
5. Flatten each piece of meat mixture in your hands to start with, then fold and smooth the meat around the eggs, pinching any cracks or splits together with your fingers.

6. Roll the Scotch eggs in the breadcrumbs then fry them two or three at a time for a very few minutes, turning frequently to get them crisp and brown all over, before baking them in the oven for about 15 minutes.
7. Serve with lots of salad and crisps.

PÂTÉ EN CROÛTE

This could be a starter, part of a cold buffet or a meal in its own right with salad, and it's nowhere near as tricky and time consuming as it would be if you made the pastry yourself.

1 lb (400–500 g) streaky bacon
³⁄₄ lb (350 g) chicken livers or lambs' liver (or a mixture of both)
1 onion
1 clove of garlic
4 tbsp breadcrumbs
¹⁄₂ small glass of sherry
2 tsp French mustard
1 tsp nutmeg
Black pepper
¹⁄₂ lb (225 g) puff pastry
1 egg, beaten
Splash of milk

Method

1. Put about half the bacon and all the liver through a mincer, or pulse gradually in a food processor until the meat is lumpy and uneven in texture (like coarse pâté, in other words).

2. Add the finely chopped onion, crushed garlic, breadcrumbs, sherry, mustard, nutmeg and black pepper to the meat mixture and squish it all together with your hands.

3. Flatten the remaining bacon rashers as much as you can by stretching them gently with a blunt knife. Line a lightly oiled standard-size loaf tin with the flattened rashers, saving 2 or 3 for the top.

4. Put the pâté mixture into the tin as evenly as possible. Fold the overlapping ends of the bacon rashers across the top and put the other rashers down the middle. (It doesn't have to look too perfect; once it's wrapped in the pastry any imperfections won't show.)

5. Cover the tin tightly with a layer of foil then place in a deep-sided casserole dish half-full of hot water and bake in the oven on Gas Mark 4 (180°C) for 30–40 minutes until the meat juices are faintly pink and the pâté has shrunk away from the sides of the tin. (You could put the loaf tin straight onto a shelf in the oven rather than in a water bath, but this way stops the pâté drying out.)

6. Carefully strain off the fat and leave the pâté to cool in the tin.

7. Meanwhile, roll out the puff pastry on a floured surface to make a square that looks large enough to completely cover the pâté with a bit left over. Break the egg into a cup or small bowl and beat with a splash of milk.

8. Ease the pâté out of the tin, place upside down in the middle of the pastry and brush with beaten egg then fold the pastry over the pâté as neatly as you can, trimming the ends and sealing the joins with more of the egg mixture.

9. Turn the pâté the right way up, brush all over with egg and use the pastry trimmings to make leaves or flower shapes for

decoration, glazing again with the rest of the egg and milk.

10. Place the Pâté en Croûte on a lightly greased oven tray and bake in a hot oven, Gas Mark 6 (200°C) for about half an hour, or until the pastry is a deep golden brown. Cool for a few minutes before transferring to the fridge.

RICE SALAD

This is another good meal for using up leftover bits and pieces so alter the ingredients to suit yourself. Try prawns, tuna, smoked salmon or a mixture of all three instead of cold meat, or keep it vegetarian and add more salad ingredients such as finely chopped peppers and mushrooms.

The most important point is to cool the cooked rice quickly by straining through a colander immediately then rinsing under cold running water and refrigerating as soon as possible. (If you leave cooked rice to cool down gradually the warm starch can become a haven for nasty bacteria.) Reheat cold rice in the microwave or in a pan with very hot oil until it's piping hot.

$^1\!/_2$ lb (225 g) basmati rice
Sugar snap peas
Baby sweetcorn
Baby plum tomatoes
Leftover chicken breast meat
A few slices of cold ham
1 avocado
2 spring onions
Chives
Olive oil
Salt & pepper

Method

1. Rinse the rice and put it in a saucepan of boiling water; boil rapidly for a couple of minutes then turn the heat down low and simmer gently for about 10 minutes (don't walk away and do something else; you don't want mushy, overcooked rice).

2. Strain the cooked rice through a colander; rinse with plenty of cold water, then put the drained rice in a large bowl. Cover loosely with a clean cloth or a piece of foil. (You don't need to keep the rice in the fridge if you're planning to eat it straight away; rice salad tastes better at room temperature than chilled.)

3. *Just* cook the baby sweetcorn and sugar snap peas (preferably in the microwave) so they still have plenty of crunch, then add to the rice.

4. Chop the meat, halve the avocado and cut into chunks, then add everything to the bowl of rice with the seasoning, whichever herbs you want to use, and a little olive oil.

5. Blend everything together by stirring gently with a large metal spoon and serve.

FALAFEL

Don't try and use tinned or cooked chickpeas for this, they really do need to be fresh and raw.

1 mug of dried chickpeas
1 tbsp gram (or plain) flour
1 oz (25 g) butter
1 tsp each of: garlic salt, onion salt, coriander, cumin, parsley
$^1\!/_2$ tsp cayenne pepper
Oil

Method

1. Soak the chickpeas in a bowl of cold water overnight then rinse, drain and blend in a food processor.
2. Put the chickpeas in a bowl with the flour, spices and melted butter and leave to stand for about 20 minutes.
3. Shape the mixture into small balls with your damp hands. Don't try and use flour; it only makes a mess and stops the mixture binding properly. (Keep a small bowl of cold water on the side so you can keep wetting your hands as you go.) But if you still have trouble getting the falafel to bind, add a little more flour *to the mixture itself.* That should do the trick.
4. Meanwhile, in a large pan heat enough oil to completely cover the falafel. Deep fry for a few minutes until golden brown and drain on kitchen paper.

Tip

If you like to use fresh chickpeas, split peas, beans and lentils but keep forgetting to soak them the night before, do a whole load at the weekend then put them into labelled food bags and freeze. That way you can cook them straight from the freezer whenever you need them.

HOT TOMATO JELLY

Tomato jelly is nice chopped and served with hot sausages and rice, curried chicken, or shellfish in a thick mayonnaise-type sauce. It would also make a very low-calorie starter on its own, or as an alternative to the shredded lettuce in a prawn cocktail – and it doesn't have to be 'hot' either; if you don't like Tabasco sauce, leave it out, although I think it's a bit bland and boring without.

Alternatively, make the jelly in a ring tin then turn out onto a plate when set and fill with any of the foods mentioned above, in which case you'd better double up the quantities below as this amount of jelly probably wouldn't be enough for most ring tins.

1 tin of plum tomatoes
$1/2$ sachet of powdered gelatine
$1/4$ pint (150 ml) boiling water
Tabasco sauce
Worcestershire sauce
Celery, onion or garlic salt
1 tsp sugar
(Basil, parsley, chives, Herbes de Provence)

Method
1. Purée the tomatoes in a blender or food processor with all the other ingredients, except the gelatine.
2. Dissolve $1/2$ sachet of gelatine in $1/4$ pint (150 ml) of water, or according to the instructions on the packet. The water needs to be very hot in order to dissolve the gelatine crystals properly and the best way to do this is to make it up in a bowl over a saucepan of boiling water. Always add the gelatine to the water, not the other way round, and stir well with a fork for about a minute.
3. Pour the puréed tomatoes into a bowl and thoroughly mix in the gelatine.
4. Leave to set in the fridge for at least 2 hours.

CLASSIC SALADS

These are all timeless classic salads that often appear in various guises in the supermarket, but as they can be put together with ingredients you'll probably have at home all year round anyway, they're worth making yourself sometimes, in which case they'll have the advantage of being fresh, and you won't be wondering how many chemicals were added before the salad was sealed inside that little plastic box five days earlier ...

SALADE NIÇOISE

This is quite similar to Greek salad, which would be made with cubes of feta cheese and green peppers instead of tuna and hard-boiled eggs, and dressed with lots of lemon juice, salt and black pepper rather than herbs and vinaigrette.

1 large or 2 small tins of tuna
4–6 tomatoes
$^1/_2$ cucumber
$^1/_2$ lb (225 g) French beans
4 hard-boiled eggs
$^1/_2$ small tub of pitted black olives
$^1/_2$ tin of anchovy fillets
1 tbsp parsley
1 tbsp basil
Garlic vinaigrette

Method

1. Hard-boil the eggs for about 10 minutes while you prepare the rest of the ingredients.
2. Drain the tin(s) of tuna and flake into fairly large chunks in a large salad bowl.
3. Top and tail the French beans and cook in the microwave (or according to the instructions on the packet) then allow them to cool completely.
4. Cut the tomatoes into wedges and thinly slice the cucumber then add to the bowl with the beans and herbs.
5. Slice the cold hard-boiled eggs and add to the bowl; mix everything together gently – don't break the eggs and tuna up completely and turn the whole lot into mush.
6. Garnish with olives and anchovies cut into thin strips and arranged in a criss-cross pattern over the top. Pour a little dressing over the salad at the end and serve the remainder of the dressing separately.

WALDORF SALAD

Use plain mayonnaise, or a flavoured one (see Salad Dressings).

1 lb (400–500g) green eating apples
1 British lettuce
$\frac{1}{2}$ head of celery
2 oz (50 g) walnuts
Lemon juice
1 tsp sugar
Mayonnaise

Method

1. Wash and cut the apples into eighths then cut each piece in half. (Keep the fruit in a small bowl and sprinkle with lemon juice as you go to prevent discolouration.) When all the apples are done, sprinkle with the sugar and add a couple of tablespoons of mayonnaise to the bowl; stir then cover with a plate or a layer of cling film while you prepare the rest of the ingredients.
2. Wash the lettuce and break it up with your hands, but not too small – and don't cut it with a knife or the leaves will discolour around the edges and quickly go limp.
3. Top and tail the celery and cut into thin slices, removing any loose strands.
4. Halve the walnuts then mix with the celery, adding both to the apples with some more mayonnaise.
5. Line a large glass bowl with the lettuce and pile the apple, celery and walnut mixture in the middle.
6. Garnish with a few crushed walnuts and serve.

CAESAR SALAD

You can buy commercially prepared croûtons in the supermarket, but making your own is so simple and such a good way of using up stale bread, it's worth doing at home at least some of the time. The bread needs to be stale because fresh bread doesn't hold its shape and absorbs too much oil. (Add garlic salt to hot oil or use a flavoured oil rather than plain vegetable or sunflower oil.) Alternatively, break up a few breadsticks, crispbakes or French toasts to use as croûtons instead.

Caesar salad can be especially good with a ripe avocado, halved and cubed, or cold, leftover chicken cut into chunks.

1 iceberg lettuce
3–4 slices of stale (white) bread
1 oz (25 g) Parmesan cheese
Lemon juice
2 cloves of garlic
Oil, plus olive oil

Method
1. Warm a mixture of oil (corn, sunflower or vegetable) and olive oil in a frying pan with the crushed garlic while you remove the crusts from the slices of stale bread and cut them into small chunks.
2. Fry the bread over a medium heat, turning every now and again until the croûtons are golden all over.
3. Meanwhile, wash and thoroughly dry the lettuce – wrap it in a clean tea towel and shake it outside or over the bath if you haven't got a salad spinner – and shred it as finely as you can.
4. Put the lettuce in a large glass bowl; sprinkle with lemon juice and mix with the croûtons – plus any other ingredients you're using – then top with the finely grated Parmesan cheese. Serve chilled.

SALAD DRESSINGS

BASIC VINAIGRETTE (FRENCH DRESSING)

4 tbsp olive oil
   or 2 tbsp each of olive oil and another 'bland' oil, e.g. corn,
   sunflower or groundnut
2 tbsp vinegar (ideally, cider or white wine)
1 tsp mustard (Dijon, French or English)
Salt & pepper

Method
Place all ingredients in a cup or small bowl and mix well with a
teaspoon, or put everything in a jar with the lid on and give it a
good shake.

Mustard Vinaigrette: To the basic recipe add an extra teaspoon of
mustard, i.e. wholegrain mustard.
Garlic Vinaigrette: To the basic recipe add 2 cloves of crushed garlic.
Hot Vinaigrette: To the basic recipe add 1–2 tsp of Tabasco sauce.
Herby Vinaigrette: To the basic recipe add 1 tbsp of chopped,
ideally fresh, herbs such as basil, flat leaf parsley, thyme or mint.
Cheesy Vinaigrette: To the basic recipe add approximately 1 oz (25
g) of crumbled blue cheese or Roquefort.

MAYONNAISE

The cheaper, paler olive oils are best for making mayonnaise, as their milder flavour won't mask the taste of the food the mayonnaise is served with. Alternatively, use corn oil or groundnut oil, or a mixture of olive oil and one of the cheaper, bland oils.

3 egg yolks
$^1/_2$ pint (300 ml) oil
3–4 tbsp cider vinegar
2 tbsp lemon juice
$^1/_2$ tsp English mustard
Salt & white pepper

Method
1. Separate the eggs and put the yolks in a cold bowl with the mustard, salt and white pepper; mix the vinegar and lemon juice together in a cup.
2. Beat the egg yolks for a minute then start adding the oil, drop by drop, to prevent the eggs curdling. Once the mayonnaise starts to thicken the oil can be added in a steady stream – but don't stop beating. (As always, it's better to use an electric hand whisk.)
3. Add half the vinegar and lemon juice as soon as the mayonnaise starts getting too thick to handle easily then carry on adding the rest of the oil.
4. Beat the rest of the vinegar and lemon juice in – the mayonnaise should be thick and smooth – and adjust the seasoning, adding more vinegar if you like a runnier texture (although this makes it salad cream rather than mayonnaise).

To rescue curdled mayonnaise

Put 1 teaspoon each of hot water and vinegar into a clean bowl and add the curdled mayonnaise a little at a time, beating continuously until the sauce is smooth. (If the mayonnaise curdled while you were making it, once it's smooth again you can carry on adding the oil a few drops at a time until it's finished.) Alternatively, try gradually beating the curdled mayonnaise into a couple of tablespoons of ready-made mayonnaise.

Lemon and mustard mayo: Mix 1 teaspoon of mustard and lemon juice according to taste with approximately 4 tablespoons of mayonnaise.

Pink mayonnaise (otherwise known as Marie Rose sauce): Add 1 teaspoon of tomato ketchup and $\frac{1}{2}$ teaspoon of paprika to $\frac{1}{4}$ pint (150 ml) of mayonnaise.

Spinach mayonnaise: Put a handful of fresh spinach into a very little boiling water then drain and either purée the spinach with a hand blender or just chop it finely. Stir into about $\frac{1}{4}$ pint (150 ml) of mayonnaise with some chopped, fresh parsley.

Cucumber and yoghurt mayonnaise: Purée or finely chop $\frac{1}{4}$ peeled cucumber; mix with roughly $\frac{1}{4}$ pint (150 ml) of mayonnaise and a couple of tablespoons of natural yoghurt.

Tip

Instead of using straight mayonnaise, mix tinned tuna or minced leftover chicken with natural yoghurt or soft cream cheese blended with a tablespoon of horseradish, wholegrain mustard or pesto for sandwiches and salads.

"Cauliflower is nothing but cabbage with a college education."

Mark Twain

CREDIT CRUNCH CUISINE

I'm not sure exactly which ingredients a recipe should contain or how it ought to be cooked and served to be worthy of the title 'cuisine', but I'd say the meals in this section fit the bill well enough for those times when you've got champagne tastes and a lemonade budget – and I didn't know where else to put them ...

BEEF TERIYAKI

You could just as easily make this with quick-frying steak (sometimes known as minute steak) but even after hammering the meat and marinating for several hours it's not always as tender as I'd like it to be, whereas a good result is guaranteed with frozen Quorn beef-style pieces – and it keeps the vegetarians happy.

Honey is more often used in teriyaki recipes, but the black treacle adds a depth and sweetness of its own (not to mention a healthy dose of iron) so give it a try, or use only half the given amount of treacle with a spoonful of honey if you're really not sure.

For more than four people use two packets of Quorn pieces with the same amount of marinade.

1–2 packets of Quorn beef-style pieces
   (*or* 4 large thin beef steaks)
1 tbsp black treacle
$^1/_2$ glass of sherry
Soy sauce
1 tsp mustard
1 tsp ginger
2 cloves of crushed garlic
Butter

Method

1. Put all the ingredients (except the Quorn and butter) in a bowl and stir with a fork for a couple of minutes to liquidize the treacle and get everything well mixed.
2. If you're using fresh beef, cut it into strips and put them in a casserole dish then pour the marinade over the meat, cover with a lid and keep in the fridge for at least 4–6 hours, and preferably overnight.
3. For the frozen Quorn method, warm some butter in a large pan and cook the beef-style pieces from frozen for about 5 minutes before adding the sauce.
4. Bring the sauce to the boil and simmer gently for a few more minutes, or for as long as it takes to cook some rice.
5. Serve with egg-fried rice and fresh green beans.

CHICKEN NOODLE BROTH

With a bit of imagination and a large packet of stir-fry vegetables from the supermarket you can (almost) recreate the Wagamama experience in your own kitchen …

Use a stock cube if that's all you've got, but this is another one of those recipes that tastes much better with fresh chicken stock. I also use a very large saucepan rather than a wok so I can cook all the chicken in one hit. Woks work brilliantly for smaller amounts of food but they're not always practical when you're cooking for a family and you want to make a larger stir-fry without cooking the meat in several batches or losing half the food over the side because the wok's not big enough to hold everything.

2–4 boneless chicken fillets
1 large packet of stir-fry vegetables
1 red chilli
1 green chilli
1 tsp ginger
1 tsp 5 Spice
A handful each of cashew nuts and sesame seeds
³⁄₄ pint (450 ml) chicken stock
Soy sauce
Lime juice
3 lumps of dried noodles
Oil

Method
1. Remove the chicken skin, trim any fatty bits if necessary and cut the meat into strips. De-seed and thinly slice the chillies.
2. Warm the pan then add the oil with the ginger, 5 Spice, chillies and sesame seeds, stirring well.
3. Cook the chicken strips in the hot oil, turning often and making sure the meat is well coated in the spicy oil.
4. Add the stir-fry vegetables and cashew nuts to the pan followed by the soy sauce and lime juice (according to taste) and give it a good stir.
5. Pour the stock into the pan, turn the heat right up and bring to the boil, then break up the noodles and add them to the stir-fry.
6. Cook for a very few minutes until the noodles are just soft, stirring frequently.
7. Eat the stir-fry as it is or serve with plain boiled rice.

CHINESE RED ROAST PORK

As long as you remember to marinate the pork the night before, this makes a lovely uncomplicated week night dinner with egg-fried rice or noodles and green vegetables.

1 ¹/₂–2 lb (750 g–1 kg) pork fillet
2 cloves of garlic, crushed
2 tbsp tomato purée
2 tbsp hoisin sauce
2 tbsp soy sauce
2 tbsp sherry
1 tbsp runny honey
2 tsp brown sugar
¹/₂ tsp 5 Spice

Method
1. Cut the lean pork into strips and make the marinade with the rest of the ingredients. (The quantities of everything in the list are approximate so start with these and adjust them a little to suit yourself if you want to.)
2. Mix the pork strips with the marinade and keep covered in the fridge for at least four hours and preferably overnight.
3. To cook the pork, preheat the oven to Gas Mark 4–5 (180–190°C) and fill a large grill pan with about ¹/₂ in (1.25 cm) of water with the rack on top.
4. Put the pork strips on the rack (with the water underneath but not touching the meat), reserve the leftover marinade and roast the pork in the oven for 30–40 minutes, or until the meat is completely tender, brushing with more marinade once or twice during the cooking time.

FRESH MACKEREL WITH LEMON & PARSLEY STUFFING

Fresh whole mackerel has always been very good value for money (as are mackerel fillets and smoked mackerel) although this recipe could work equally well with rainbow trout, which is a bit more expensive but still affordable.

4 fresh whole mackerel
Lemon juice
2 bay leaves
Black pepper
Salt

For the stuffing
1 onion
4 heaped tbsp breadcrumbs
1 lemon (finely grated rind and juice)
1 tbsp parsley
1 egg yolk
Butter

Method
1. Melt a lump of butter in a pan and fry the finely chopped onion till just golden.
2. Mix the onion with the breadcrumbs, parsley, egg yolk and the finely grated rind and juice of one whole lemon.
3. Open up the mackerel and season the fish with black pepper, salt and more lemon juice then fill each one with the stuffing and place in a lightly buttered ovenproof dish with a very little water (just enough to cover the bottom of the dish).

4. Put the bay leaves in the water and cover the dish with a lid or a loose layer of foil and cook in the oven on Gas Mark 3 (170°C) for about 20 minutes, until the fish is tender but not falling apart.
5. Serve with new potatoes or fried potatoes and a tomato salad.

ROASTED VEGETABLES WITH RED ONION & ROQUEFORT

You could use another cheese for this, but although Roquefort is more expensive than your everyday Cheddar you only need a little to add a lot of flavour, so it's more than worth it. (Or try a bit of English Stilton if you prefer.)

This could be a side dish, or a vegetarian main course with salad and garlic bread.

For the roasted vegetables
1 large butternut squash
3–4 mixed peppers
4–5 carrots
2 onions
1 tin of chopped tomatoes
Olive oil

For the topping
1 red onion
4 big tbsp of porridge oats
2 oz (50 g) Roquefort
Olive oil

Method

1. Cut the butternut squash in half; peel the skin with a potato peeler, remove the pips and the foamy inner bit and cut into wedges.
2. Top and tail the carrots, scrape and thinly slice diagonally (long thin carrots are best for this). Halve the peppers, de-seed and cut into strips; peel and slice the onions.
3. Put the vegetables into a large ovenproof dish, drizzle with olive oil and bake in the oven on Gas Mark 6 (200°C) for 20–25 minutes or until the vegetables are roasted and golden brown.
4. Meanwhile, warm some more olive oil in a frying pan and cook the finely chopped red onion for a few minutes before adding the porridge oats to the pan. (Cook for a few more minutes until the oats colour up a bit, if you like – or not. As long as the oats are incorporated into the oil and onions it doesn't really matter.)
5. Crumble the cheese into the pan with the oats and onions and mix well.
6. Take the roasted vegetables out of the oven and pour over the chopped tomatoes.
7. Spread the red onion and Roquefort topping all over the surface, turn the oven up to Gas Mark 7 (220°C) and put the roasted vegetables back in for another 10–15 minutes.

FILO PASTRY PIE

This is yet another one of those recipes that impresses your friends and in no way reflects the complete lack of effort involved. (In other words, the best kind.)

This pie should ideally be made in one large spring-release cake tin; it's quite delicate and you don't want it collapsing completely when you take it out. However, even though I am actually the proud owner of two spring-release cake tins (also several loose-bottomed ones) I nearly always make two smaller pies in the same standard-size sandwich tins I'd normally use for baking sponge cakes.

To get the pies out of the tins I either put a plate over the top of each one, turning it out upside down then putting a plate over it again and turning it the right way up, or – if I think I can get away with it – quickly tipping the pie straight out onto the palm of my hand, then onto the plate.

The other good thing about making two smaller pies is you can alter the fillings slightly, and use whichever kind of crumbly white cheese you want (I like feta) or a mixture of hard cheeses, according to what you've got.

1 packet of large filo pastry sheets ($^1/_2$ lb+/250g = roughly 16 sheets)
$^1/_2$ bag of baby leaf spinach
3 good-size courgettes
1 or 2 tomatoes
1 big tbsp red pesto
1 tsp nutmeg
1 tsp coriander
Cumin seeds
Salt & pepper
Olive oil
Butter
Crumbly cheese (feta, ricotta, Roquefort, goats' cheese)

Method

1. Warm some olive oil in a saucepan while you cut the courgettes into thin slices, halving or quartering the slices according to how you want them to be.

2. Put the cumin seeds in the pan and fry for a minute before adding the courgettes, cook for a few more minutes until the courgettes have softened then add some coriander and stir in the pesto.

3. Take the pan off the heat and leave the courgettes to cool a little while you wash and tear up the spinach leaves and finely slice the tomatoes.

4. Preheat the oven to Gas Mark 6 (200°C) and melt about 1 oz (25 g) of butter in the microwave. Brush the cake tin or tins and arrange 5–6 sheets of pastry at the bottom, brushing each one with butter and overlapping them, leaving the excess hanging over the edge of the tin all the way round.

5. Put the courgettes in first, followed by a layer of spinach; sprinkle with nutmeg then add a layer of sliced tomatoes seasoned with salt and pepper.

6. Crumble the cheese (however much feels right to you) over the tomatoes then fold the overhanging pastry layers across the top, again brushing each sheet with the melted butter as you go.

7. If you want more pastry on the top, break up another couple of sheets and crumple them up on top of the pie, or pies, brush with the remaining butter, and bake in the oven for about 20 minutes until the pastry is crisp and golden.

8. Serve with salad or salad and rice.

CAULIFLOWER CHEESE SOUFFLÉ

This is the only unsinkable soufflé recipe I know, so it's the only one I ever make. If you like you can add thinly sliced courgettes, onions or mushrooms – or all three – to the cauliflower to make it more of a main course in its own right, or just serve it as a side dish with a meaty dinner and potatoes. It's lighter than regular cauliflower cheese and looks good too, so give it a go.

1 cauliflower
1 oz (25 g) butter or margarine
2–3 tbsp flour
$^{1}\!/_{2}$ pint (250 ml) milk
3 eggs, separated
1–2 oz (25–50 g) Cheddar cheese
1–2 oz (25–50 g) Parmesan cheese

Method
1. Cut the cauliflower into florets and simmer gently in a saucepan of boiling water (or steam) for a few minutes until slightly softened but nowhere near mushy. Transfer the cauliflower to a soufflé dish and preheat the oven to Gas Mark 4 (180°C).
2. Melt the butter or margarine in a saucepan and stir in the flour. (There's a bit more flour to margarine than usual in this recipe so the paste will be very thick at this stage; you really should use a whisk to get rid of any lumps when you add the milk.)
3. Add the milk and grated Cheddar cheese together and whisk continuously with a small or medium-sized balloon whisk for a few minutes until you have a thick, smooth sauce.

4. Remove the pan from the heat and whisk the egg yolks into the cheese sauce.

5. Whisk the egg whites in a separate bowl until stiff then thoroughly fold into the cheese sauce with a large metal spoon and pour the sauce over the cauliflower in the soufflé dish.

6. Sprinkle the finely grated Parmesan cheese over the surface and bake in the oven for 20–25 minutes, until the soufflé is ever so slightly risen and golden on top.

CALVES' LIVER IN SHERRY SAUCE

Although calves' liver is considerably more expensive than any other kind it's well worth it sometimes, not only for its lovely smooth texture and subtle flavour, but because it cooks really quickly and there's virtually no preparation involved.

This is delicious served with creamy mashed potatoes and spinach.

Calves' liver
Baby onions or shallots
$^1/_2$ pint (250 ml) beef stock
$^1/_4$ pint (125 ml) apple juice
$^1/_4$ pint (125 ml) sherry
Balsamic vinegar
1 tbsp flour
1 tsp salt
Butter

Method

1. Warm some butter in a large, deep-sided pan while you peel the onions or shallots. Cut into quarters then fry gently for a few minutes until soft.
2. Sift in the flour and cook for another minute.
3. Stir in the beef stock and apple juice, bring to the boil and reduce slightly before stirring in the sherry, a splash of balsamic vinegar and a teaspoon of salt.
4. Keep the sauce warm while you fry the liver in more butter in another pan for a couple of minutes on each side; the liver should still be soft and pink on the inside.
5. Serve with mashed potatoes mixed with a couple of spoonfuls of herby soft cream cheese, and any green vegetable.

ORIENTAL BEEF WITH LIME DUMPLINGS

You could get away with using lime juice instead of fresh lime, but the lime zest in the dumplings is what gives them their special fragrance. (Or you could try mixing the flour and suet with lime juice instead of water, I suppose.)

If you want to make this in advance, take the stew out of the oven and let it cool down as soon as the beef is tender then reheat thoroughly, adding the spring greens and dumplings once the stock is simmering gently.

2 lb (1 kg) stewing beef
1 bunch of spring onions
2 cloves of garlic
2–2 ½ pints (1–1½ litres) beef stock
1 glass of sherry
Soy sauce

2 fresh limes
2–3 tsp ginger
2 tsp sugar
Spring greens
8 oz (225 g) self-raising flour
4 oz (100 g) suet
Black pepper
Oil
Water

Method

1. Warm plenty of oil in a large saucepan while you trim the meat, season with black pepper and coat with a little flour. (You'd normally use plain flour, but as you need self-raising flour for the dumplings you may as well use that instead. I can't see that it makes any difference.)
2. Quickly brown the meat in batches, transferring it to a large casserole dish as you go, then add the chopped spring onions and garlic to the pan with the sugar and ginger and fry for a couple of minutes.
3. Put the onions and garlic in the casserole dish with the meat then add the juice from the limes with the sherry, the stock and plenty of soy sauce and give the stew a good stir.
4. Cover with a lid and cook in a very low oven, Gas Mark 2 (150–160ºC), for about 2–2 ½ hours until the meat is just tender.
5. Meanwhile, finely grate the lime zest (if you haven't already) and keep it covered in the fridge for later.
6. When the stew is ready, make the dumplings by mixing the flour, suet and lime zest in a bowl and combining with 3–4 tbsp of water to make a smooth, slightly sticky dough. Roll the dough into small balls with your hands.

7. Wash and shred the spring greens then stir into the stew. Put the dumplings on the top and push them down a bit, and if you think there's not quite enough liquid in the stew by this stage, add a little cold water to thin it out before you add the dumplings.

8. Turn the oven up to Gas Mark 5–6 (190–200ºC), put the stew back in and cook for approximately 15 minutes until the dumplings are puffed up and slightly golden. Perfect with green beans and egg-fried rice.

RAVIOLI

Making your own pasta is a fun thing to do sometimes and a lot less hassle than you might think – even when you don't have a pasta-making machine. The hardest bit is rolling out the dough because at first it keeps springing back, but the process gets easier as you go along, so grit your teeth for a couple of minutes and try and think of it as a great, free toning exercise for the upper body.

This probably isn't something you'd want to get into after a busy day at work; otherwise it's well worth having a go at least once. Chances are you'll be hooked, and before you know it you'll be buying a machine and making your own pasta all the time ...

You could cut the finished pasta into strips or lasagne sheets, in which case it's best to use the pasta straight away to stop it welding itself together, but I think it's actually easier and certainly more rewarding to make ravioli, not only because it looks and tastes better, but because it can be stored in a food bag in the fridge for a couple of days without getting too sticky.

Super-fine 00 flour is perfect for making pasta but I always get a good result with ordinary plain flour; just be sure to sift the whole lot at least once before you start. It's also important to follow the instructions carefully in the early stages when you're incorporating the eggs and spinach purée into the flour. You won't need to use all the flour to make the dough, as you'll see, so don't work too quickly and risk pulling more flour into the mixture than you need or the pasta will be ruined and you won't be able to do a thing about it.

Although the spinach gives this ravioli a lovely colour and flavour of its own, if you want yellow pasta instead of green, leave out the spinach purée and use four large eggs instead of three.

Finally, the amounts given here are enough for about eight servings so you could store half the dough in the fridge for a couple of days, then when you're ready to use the pasta let it rest at room temperature for a couple of hours and knead it gently for a few minutes before rolling it out again.

3 full mugs of flour (00 or plain)
3 large eggs
1–2 handfuls of spinach
Tomato purée
Ricotta (or feta) cheese
Salt

Method

1. Wash and tear the spinach, place in a small casserole dish with a very little water then cover with a lid and cook in the microwave for about 2 minutes until the leaves have wilted. Purée the cooked spinach in a blender or food processor.
2. Now sift the flour into a big heap on a clean work surface, or straight onto a very large wooden board, and make a deep well in the centre.
3. Break the eggs into the well one at a time then add about half the spinach purée and use a blunt dinner knife to gently work

the flour in a little at a time, taking care not to send the liquid cascading over the edge of the flour and all over the worktop.

4. Work carefully, adding a little more of the spinach purée if it looks like the mixture can take it, then once you've got the beginnings of a soft dough, gather the remaining flour together and sift it back onto your work surface in a neat pile so you're working with clean, new flour again. (This step should take around 5 minutes.)

5. Re-flour your work surface, adding a little more flour to the dough as and when you need it to prevent it becoming too sticky.

6. Knead the dough for about 15 minutes, pushing the dough away from you with the heels of your hands, until the dough becomes pliable and springy. Test by pressing the dough with your finger; if the dent disappears and the dough regains its shape, it's ready.

7. Wrap the dough in cling film, or cover it with an up-turned bowl and allow it to rest for 20–30 minutes at room temperature.

8. Roll the dough out with a large rolling pin, turning frequently and adding a little more flour when necessary, until the dough is as thin as you can make it without breaking it and you can see the shadow of your hand through it.

9. Use a large pastry cutter with a fluted edge – or an ordinary mug if you don't have one – to cut out as many rounds as you can. Put the pasta rounds on a lightly floured tray while you re-roll the trimmings, lightly kneading the dough a bit more each time to keep it malleable without overworking it.

10. Squeeze a pea-sized amount of tomato purée onto the centre of each piece of pasta, top with $1/2$ teaspoon of cheese and fold the rounds into semi-circles, pressing the edges together to seal the ravioli. (Don't try and use water to help seal the edges as

you would with pastry; this makes the pasta too tacky without actually sticking it together for some reason.)

11. Cook the ravioli in a large saucepan of salted boiling water for about 3 minutes and serve with grated fresh Parmesan cheese and a side salad.
12. To store in the fridge, dust the ravioli with a little flour and put in a large food bag, or on a plate covered with cling film.

PASTA WITH HOME-MADE PESTO

As long as you've got a food processor, making your own pesto is a doddle; the quantities for each of these recipes will fill a jam jar and keep in the fridge for about a week.

It's hard to be more precise about the amount of oil you need to use; I've said $^1/_4$ pint (125 ml) each time, so add the oil very slowly until you think the pesto has reached the right consistency. (You probably won't need this much.)

Swap the ingredients around to suit yourself, try different flavoured oils and use whichever combination of nuts, seeds and herbs you like.

Olive & Parsley Seed Pesto

4 oz (100 g) mixed seeds
$^1/_2$ small tub of mixed pitted olives
1 packet (30 g) of fresh, flat leaf parsley
1 oz (25 g) Parmesan cheese
1 tbsp tomato purée
$^1/_2$ tbsp garlic purée
Lemon juice

Black pepper
¹/₄ pint (125 ml) olive oil

Method
1. Wash the fresh parsley, cut the stalks off, then tear up and put in the food processor with the seeds, olives, grated Parmesan, tomato and garlic purées.
2. Season with black pepper and a little lemon juice then whiz for a minute, stopping to scrape the food away from the sides every few seconds.
3. Add the olive oil gradually through the funnel with the food processor on pulse or the slowest setting, until it looks right to you.
4. Pack the pesto into a clean jar and pour another 2 tsp of olive oil on top.
5. Store in the fridge for a week.

Aubergine Pesto

This is one recipe with aubergines where you don't have to worry about how much oil they absorb in the cooking process because the pesto incorporates the same oil you've used for frying.

3 oz (75 g) mixed nuts and seeds
1 oz (25 g) flax seeds
1 small aubergine
2 cloves of garlic
1 sprig of rosemary
¹/₂ packet of fresh mint
1 oz (25 g) grated Parmesan
1 tbsp tomato purée

Black pepper
$^1/_4$ pint (125 ml) olive oil

Method

1. Cut the aubergine into fairly thick slices and soak in a bowl of very salty water for about 20 minutes, then drain, rinse well and dry with kitchen paper.
2. Heat half the quantity of oil in a large frying pan and preheat the oven to Gas Mark 6 (200ºC).
3. Fry half the aubergine slices in the hot oil for a few minutes, turning once, then transfer to a small roasting tin. Add the remaining oil to the pan and fry the rest of the aubergine, again transferring the cooked aubergine to the roasting tin.
4. Snip the rosemary up and sprinkle over the aubergine then add the crushed garlic to the roasting tin and put it in the oven for 20–25 minutes until the aubergines are completely soft and cooked through. All the oil that was soaked up during frying should now be swimming around in the tin.
5. Remove the tin from the oven and allow to cool for a few minutes while you get the rest of the ingredients ready then put the aubergines and all the oil into a blender or food processor with everything else and blend or pulse to make a coarse paste, scraping the pesto down from the sides every few seconds.
6. Pack the pesto into a clean jar and pour another 2 tsp of olive oil on top.
7. Store in the fridge for a week.

Red Pepper & Onion Pesto

4 oz (100 g) pine nuts
1 red pepper
1 red onion
1 packet (30 g) of fresh basil
1 oz (25 g) Parmesan
2 tbsp tomato purée
$^1/_2$ tbsp garlic purée
Black pepper
$^1/_4$ pint (125 ml) of olive oil

Method

1. Peel and chop the red onion; remove the stalk and seeds from the red pepper and cut into rough chunks.
2. Rinse the fresh basil and put the herbs in the food processor with the pine nuts, red pepper, onion, grated Parmesan and tomato and garlic purées.
3. Season with black pepper then whiz for a minute, stopping to scrape the food away from the sides every few seconds.
4. Add the olive oil gradually through the funnel with the food processor on pulse or the slowest setting, until it looks right to you.
5. Pack the pesto into a clean jam jar and pour another 2 tsp of olive oil on top.
8. Store in the fridge for a week.

Pasta with Home-made Pesto

Obviously you can use whichever type of pasta you like, but fresh tagliatelli or those super-sized dried white pasta shells are a bit more impressive than a packet of value twists if you're making this for friends.

Method

1. Bring a large saucepan of lightly salted water to the boil then add the pasta and cook according to the instructions on the packet.
2. Drain the cooked pasta, leaving a very little of the water in the pan, then add a couple of tablespoons of pesto and warm through for a minute over a very low heat.
3. Serve the pasta and pesto with more finely grated fresh Parmesan cheese and lots of salad.

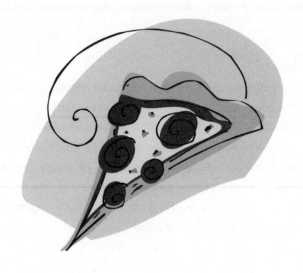

"If we don't sing the songs, tell the stories, and make the foods that are dear to us, our children won't know what they missed, but I think they'll miss it just the same."

Laura Ward Branca

KIDS' FAVOURITES

I once knew a woman whose cooking was so bad it would have been funny, except one of her children used to cry and gag his way through every meal and the other one was eventually referred to a dietician for being chronically anaemic and underweight. Her crimes in the kitchen included self-mashing potatoes that were boiled to breaking point and roast chicken with the skin removed first so the meat was even drier and chewier than it would normally have been after a whole morning (yes, a whole morning) in the oven.

Even worse, her idea of encouraging her kids to eat was to keep a wooden spoon on the table as a threat. She said she came from a family where 'children have to eat their vegetables', so she gave them overcooked meat and sloppy mash with waterlogged cabbage, mushy broccoli or rubbery carrots almost every day, occasionally replacing the potatoes with oven chips for a treat. About the only meal the poor little things could keep down was breakfast because not much can go wrong with Weetabix and cold milk, but instead of worrying about the unhappy state of her own children's diet she was deeply critical of mums who'd rather reward their kids with a small treat after dinner every day than terrorize them with a wooden spoon.

I know it's not always easy to produce something your children will happily eat and which is also good for them, especially if you have more than one fussy little eater in your house, but there's still so much available, affordable food to choose from these days, it's virtually impossible not to find something your kids will like, as long as you're prepared to give it your all and be patient.

And if you can't please all of the children all of the time, try letting them each have a turn at choosing what to have for dinner, on the strict understanding that this only works if everyone goes along with it. (The alternative is, you decide what they eat every single day and the children don't have any say at all.)

As far as I'm concerned it's perfectly okay to resort to any amount of good-natured bribery and blackmail to get your children to eat the right foods, but it's a one-way street, meaning you're not obliged to give in to their demands for vile processed lunchables, chocolate jammy dipper things and fizzy drinks – at least not on a daily basis – which seems to me like avoiding a tantrum now and risking a heart attack later on.

Having said that, I also think it's a good idea to let them have all these things occasionally so they're never made to feel deprived or different from their friends, which, understandably, is nothing short of a disaster for most children.

I read a newspaper article not long ago by a mother who said she regretted feeding her children a pure, unadulterated, organic diet because they'd become hyper-critical little foodies with impossibly high standards, meaning she never had a chance to relax the rules and fob them off with a jam sandwich – which may not be as bad as having a child who eats only jam sandwiches, but still, who needs it?

Luckily, feeding your children doesn't have to be a nightmare, so try and be relaxed about it. You don't have to stick to a rigid, albeit healthy, routine of 'five a day' every day (and counting) with no allowances for parties and pyjama days, but nor do you have to give up altogether and go to Iceland ... .at least not all the time. There's plenty of room in between those two extremes, and finding your own happy medium isn't as hard as all that.

One of the wisest and truest pieces of advice I was given when my own kids were small was that children can only afford to be as fussy with their food as their parents will let them, so keep on trying new things and recycling old favourites. That way you'll quickly find out what works best in your house, and before you know it, everyone will be eating everything you give them virtually all the time, and at least one area of your life will be relatively stress-free.

CHICKEN CURRY

This is a really good little curry for young children. Mild, creamy and made only with vegetables in child-friendly colours it also includes sweetcorn, which is one of the few foods (like pasta, potatoes and yoghurt) that almost all children seem to eat without question.

Once your kids are hooked on this you can start sneaking in the spinach. (Don't add extra sugar if you don't want to, especially if the orange juice is a sweet one.)

2–4 chicken fillets
1 onion
4 carrots
1 large sweet potato
1 tin of sweetcorn
1 small carton of natural yoghurt (or 4 tbsp from a big carton)
1 sachet of coconut or $\frac{1}{2}$ tin of coconut milk
1 mug of orange juice
1 big tbsp tomato purée
2 tsp mild curry powder (or 1 tsp medium)
1 tsp cumin
1 tsp coriander
$\frac{1}{4}$ tsp ginger
1 tsp sugar

Method
1. Wash and finely slice the carrots; peel the sweet potato, cut into largish chunks and grate the onion.
2. Cut the chicken into thin strips while you warm some oil in a large pan.

3. Cook the chicken strips a few at a time unless the pan is big enough to take the whole lot, in which case, cook all the chicken in one go. (The meat won't brown if the pan is full, but it doesn't matter with this recipe.)
4. Add the grated onion, sugar and spices to the pan and cook for a couple more minutes, making sure the chicken is well coated.
5. Add the carrot slices and sweet potato chunks followed by the orange juice, yoghurt, coconut milk and tomato purée; stir well, cover with a lid and cook over a low heat for about 40 minutes, or until the vegetables are just soft.
6. Adjust the seasoning and consistency and serve with couscous, rice, chips or mashed potatoes (yes, really).

CHICKEN NUGGETS

Most kids seem to love chicken nuggets and they're a brilliant way of making a little good-quality meat go a very long way. You can expect to make at least a couple of dozen nuggets with the quantities given here.

2 chicken fillets
2 carrots
2 apples
1 onion
1 lb (450 g) breadcrumbs
Tarragon
Salt & pepper
1 egg
Splash of milk

Method

1. Wash and roughly chop the carrots and onion, peel and core the apples, remove the skin from the chicken and cut the meat into large pieces.

2. Put carrots, onion, apples and chicken into a large (4 pint/2 litre) blender or food processor with the tarragon, salt and pepper – or whatever seasoning you prefer.

3. If you're using the above quantities, blend the whole lot in one go on the slowest setting to the consistency you want – anything from coarse and chunky to a smooth paste – and if you've got a smaller food processor or you're making twice as many nuggets, blend the chicken first, followed by the fruit and vegetables. (If you haven't got a mixer you can always grate the fruit and vegetables by hand and snip the chicken into tiny pieces with kitchen scissors.)

4. Put the blended ingredients into a large bowl and squish it all together with your hands, adding a handful of breadcrumbs if you think the mixture's a bit wet.

5. Spread the breadcrumbs across a large, shallow dish or tray and beat the egg with a big splash of milk.

6. Now shape the nuggets with your hands, dipping each one into the egg mixture first, and working with only a small amount of breadcrumbs at a time to avoid making a mess of the whole tray and creating too much waste.

7. In a large pan warm enough oil to completely submerge the nuggets (about 2 inches/5 cm) and test if it's hot enough by dropping a small chunk of bread into the pan; it should go brown in a matter of seconds. If the oil is too cool the nuggets will break up and go soggy; if it's just right they should turn crisp and golden in about a minute.

8. Fry the nuggets for a couple of minutes then place on a baking tray and finish them off in the oven on Gas Mark 5 (190°C) for about 15 minutes to cook through.

To freeze chicken nuggets

1. Place uncooked chicken nuggets on a small tray, cover with foil and seal in a freezer bag, or layer with greaseproof paper in a plastic container with a tight lid.
2. To cook them from frozen, first allow the nuggets to thaw slightly for a few minutes so they're easier to separate, then remove excess moisture with kitchen roll and, for best results, follow the cooking instructions above.

Tip
Foil takeaway cartons (as long as they're really clean) can be reused for freezing and cooking smaller portions of food in the oven, as can 'disposable' roasting trays.

TANDOORI CHICKEN

This is enough for at least eight large chicken joints; more if you're using thighs and drumsticks.

Chicken pieces
$^1/_2$ large pot (500 g) of natural yoghurt
2 tsp curry powder
2 tsp coriander
2 tsp paprika
$^1/_2$ tsp chilli powder
Lemon or lime juice to taste
Salt & pepper

Method

1. Wash chicken, remove skin and score several deep cuts in each piece of meat.
2. Mix all ingredients together and coat the chicken pieces thoroughly then cover and keep in the fridge to marinate for at least 4 hours, or even overnight.
3. Transfer the chicken to a clean ovenproof dish and bake in the oven on Gas Mark 5 (190°C) for about half an hour, turning once.
4. Serve with rice.

SOUTHERN FRIED CHICKEN

This is the seasoning the way I like it but you can make it hotter or milder by adjusting the amount of spices and herbs any way you like.

Southern fried chicken the way they make it in America would be double-dipped in buttermilk, beaten egg and two coatings of seasoned breadcrumbs, but either one of the following methods works well: either dunk the chicken in a mixture of beaten egg and milk before coating with the breadcrumbs, or dip the chicken in a thin batter made with plain flour, beaten egg and milk, *then* coat with breadcrumbs. (I prefer the latter because the breadcrumbs stick better this way.)

The quantities below are enough for 12 pieces of chicken.

Chicken pieces (12)

For the seasoning
1 tbsp paprika
1 teaspoon each of: cayenne pepper, onion salt, garlic salt, celery

salt, allspice, chilli powder, black pepper, basil, thyme, marjoram
4 oz (100 g) breadcrumbs
4 tbsp cornmeal or yellow maize flour

For the batter
3 tbsp plain flour
1 egg
1 mug of milk (approximately)
(Plus more flour for dusting)

Oil for frying

Method
1. Remove all chicken skin, trim any fatty pieces, rinse chicken in cold water and dry the meat thoroughly.
2. Mix all the spices and herbs with the breadcrumbs and cornmeal in a large deep-sided dish or tray and dust the dry chicken pieces with a little flour.
3. Make a thin batter with plain flour, egg and milk by making a well in the flour then beating in the egg with about half the milk and gradually adding more milk to get the right consistency.
4. Warm enough oil in a very large pan to completely cover the chicken (or use an electric deep-fat fryer) and preheat the oven to Gas Mark 5 (190°C).
5. Dip the chicken pieces in the thin batter then cover completely with the breadcrumb mixture.
6. Fry the chicken pieces 3 or 4 at a time for a couple of minutes until the coating is crisp and golden, then finish in the oven for about 15 minutes, or until the meat is cooked through.
7. Serve with chips or rice and salad.

STICKY RIBS

This should be enough for two large packets of small pork ribs. You can also use this marinade to coat chicken drumsticks and sausages.

Pork ribs
$^1/_2$ pint (300 ml) tomato juice
2 tbsp vinegar
2 tbsp clear honey
1 tsp paprika

Method
1. Mix the tomato juice, vinegar, honey and paprika together using all the marinade to coat the ribs then cover and keep in the fridge for at least two hours.
2. Cook the ribs under a high, preheated grill for about 20 minutes, turning once or twice and re-coating the meat with the marinade each time.
3. Serve with new potatoes or rice and salad.

JAMAICA PATTIES

You should get about a dozen patties out of the quantities below, depending on the size of the plate you use to cut out the pastry.

Like most other pies and pasties these make a great alternative to sandwiches for a packed lunch – that is, until primary schools with 'healthy schools status' decide to ban pastry from the children's lunch boxes on the grounds that it contains more calories than wholemeal bread. (Well it wouldn't surprise me. That's how daft some of these new rules and regulations are.)

For the pastry
1 lb (500 g) plain flour
1 tbsp turmeric (or 1 sachet from a refill box)
¹⁄₂ lb (225 g) butter
³⁄₄ mug ice-cold water
1 beaten egg (plus water)

For the filling
1 lb (500 g) beef mince
2 onions
2 cloves of garlic
1 heaped tsp chilli powder (or less!)
2 tsp curry powder
2 tbsp tomato purée
1 beef stock cube

Method
1. Sift the flour and turmeric into a large mixing bowl and slightly soften the butter in the microwave (on defrost for about 30 seconds) then add the butter to the bowl in small pieces and rub the fat into the flour until it resembles medium-fine breadcrumbs.
2. Add about half the cold water to the mixture in the bowl and pinch the mixture together with your hands to make a fairly stiff dough, adding a little more water if necessary.
3. Put the dough in a polythene food bag or wrap it in cling film and leave it to rest in the fridge while you get on with the filling.

4. Dry fry the mince in a large pan while you finely chop the onions, then add them to the pan and cook for a few minutes until the meat is brown and the onions have softened.

5. Strain all the fat out of the pan and dissolve the stock cube in a mug of boiling water, then add the stock to the meat followed by the chilli powder, curry powder, crushed garlic and tomato purée.

6. Stir well and allow the meat to simmer for at least 20 minutes until the sauce thickens nicely. (Adjust the sauce by adding a little more water and/or more tomato purée if you like.)

7. Allow the meat sauce to cool while you preheat the oven to Gas Mark 6 (200°C) and lightly grease two large baking sheets. Beat the egg in a mug with 3 or 4 tablespoons of cold water.

8. Divide the dough into two pieces and roll each half out, one at a time, cutting around a small side plate or saucer to make the patties and re-rolling the trimmings to make more as necessary.

9. Put roughly 1 tbsp of meat in the centre of each pastry round and use the egg/water mixture to wet the edges of the pastry.

10. Fold each pastry in half over its filling to make a semi-circular patty, pressing the edges down with a fork and piercing fork holes in the centre of each patty two or three times.

11. Glaze the patties with more of the egg/water mixture, place on the greased baking trays and cook in the oven for about 20 minutes until the pastry is firm and golden.

12. Serve hot or cold, on their own or with Cheesy Corn Fritters (see this chapter, page 153), rice and salad.

BURGERS WITH BLUE CHEESE DRESSING

Mix in a tablespoon of dried mint if you're using lamb and ½ teaspoon of cayenne pepper to either beef or lamb. Ideally, make the dressing a few hours before you need it to give the flavours a chance to develop.

To make 6 good-sized burgers
2 lb (1 kg) minced lamb or beefsteak
1 large onion, finely chopped
1 egg to bind
Seasoning

For the blue cheese dressing
3 oz (75 g) blue cheese
½ small jar of mayonnaise
1 small carton of natural yoghurt
1 clove of garlic
1 tsp lemon juice
1 tsp vinegar

Method
1. Squish everything together in a large bowl and pat the mixture into burger shapes with your hands, making them as large and thin as you can without tearing. (Don't use flour; wet your hands with cold water to make it easier.)
2. For best results put the burgers under the grill on the highest setting and cook on both sides for a few minutes until they're brown on the outside and just done in the middle.
3. Serve (with or without buns) with chips and relish.

To make the blue cheese dressing

1. Crumble the cheese into a bowl and add the mayonnaise, yoghurt and crushed garlic.
2. Mix the ingredients together before adding the lemon juice and vinegar. Stir well then taste the dressing before adjusting the flavour with a very little more lemon or vinegar, or a bit of both.

SAUSAGE & EGG MUFFINS

These are less greasy, and must be better for you than the obvious alternative, providing you make them with good-quality sausages (minimum 70% meat) and poached eggs instead of fried. I'm sure the original McMuffins had sliced tomato in them anyway, so put some in, with or instead of the cheese.

Cook the eggs in a proper poacher if you have one, to get that perfectly round shape, and make this a real weekend breakfast with the addition of home-made hash browns (see Chapter 3, under 'Potatoes').

6 muffins
6 eggs
6 sausages
1 tomato
3 slices of Emmental

Method

1. Carefully squeeze the sausages out of their skins and make each one into a flattened out round patty with your hands. (Use a very little flour if it helps, or just wet your hands with cold water.)
2. Bake the sausage patties in the oven on Gas Mark 6 (200°C)

for about 20 minutes or until you can see they're obviously cooked through.
3. Meanwhile, cut the muffins in half and lightly toast the inside. Thinly slice the tomato and cheese.
4. When the sausages are almost done, poach the eggs in a large shallow pan of boiling water for about 5 minutes, until the yolks are firm.
5. Serve with tomato ketchup.

CHILLI DOGS

In America, Chilli Dogs are made with a ground beef sauce, very similar to Chilli con Carne, so this is a lightweight version of the real thing; much less calorific and easier to eat with your hands.

Hot dog rolls
Jumbo frankfurters or large sausages
1 tin of chopped tomatoes
3–4 tbsp tomato purée
2 onions
1 clove of garlic
3–4 medium mixed red and green chillies
2 tbsp vinegar
2 tsp sugar
$^1\!/_2$ tsp salt

Method
1. De-seed and thoroughly rinse the chillies in cold water.
2. Roughly chop the chillies and onions, crush the garlic and put into a large saucepan with the chopped tomatoes, tomato purée, vinegar, sugar and salt.

3. Bring the sauce to the boil, stirring occasionally, then simmer for about 20 minutes.

4. Allow the sauce to cool slightly then whiz it in a blender or food processor.

5. Keep the sauce warm, or cool completely and refrigerate for later on. (Reheat in the microwave when needed.)

6. Cook the sausages or warm the frankfurters according to the instructions on the packet, then make several deep cuts along the length of each one with a sharp knife.

7. Put the sausages or frankfurters into rolls and spoon the sauce over the meat. (Spread the rolls with a little French or wholegrain mustard for extra flavour.)

CRAB CAKES

One small tin of crabmeat makes about 8 little crab cakes.

1½ oz (40 g) gram flour
2 oz butter or margarine
½ mug of milk
1 small (7 oz/170 g) tin of crabmeat
2 tsp 5 Spice
Chives
2 tbsp sesame seeds
1 egg
Lemon juice
Black pepper

Method

1. Drain the tin of crabmeat and season with 5 Spice, lemon juice, black pepper and chives.
2. Melt the butter or margarine in a small saucepan, beat in the sifted flour and cook for a minute, stirring continuously, then add the milk and whisk for a couple more minutes to make a very thick sauce.
3. Take the pan off the heat and add the crabmeat, sesame seeds and more lemon juice, then stir everything together and shape the mixture into small cakes with your hands.
4. Place on an oiled baking tray and bake in a hot oven, Gas Mark 6 (200°C) for 20–25 minutes and serve with a sweet chilli sauce, oven chips and salad.

Tip

Gram flour (chickpea flour) mixed to a paste with sugar or salt and lemon juice makes a good, cheap exfoliator and skin softener, as do porridge oats mixed with a little warm water. If you're addicted to brand name beauty products these home-made versions won't impress you much, but they do exactly the same job for a lot less money.

FISH FINGER PIE

Fish fingers (2–4 per person, depending on size of person)
Spinach
Tomatoes
Grated cheese

Method

1. Place fish fingers side by side in batches of 2–4 and grill on high for about 10 minutes.
2. Wash and slice the tomatoes, finely shred the spinach and grate the cheese.
3. Turn the fish fingers over and grill on the second side for no more than 2 minutes.
4. Cover each batch of fish fingers with a layer of spinach and top with the slices of tomato and grated cheese.
5. Grill for a few more minutes until the cheese is brown and bubbling.
6. Serve with chips.

CHEESY CORN FRITTERS

1 large tin of sweetcorn
1 oz (25 g) hard cheese
3 tbsp flour
1 egg
$\frac{1}{2}$ cup of milk (approx)
$\frac{1}{2}$ tsp paprika
$\frac{1}{2}$ tsp cumin
$\frac{1}{2}$ tsp coriander
Oil

Method

1. Sift the flour and spices into a mixing bowl then make a well in the centre, add the egg and half of the milk and beat it all together with a fork or small hand whisk to make a thick, smooth batter. (Add the rest of the milk if the batter's too stodgy.)

2. Grate the cheese, drain the tin of sweetcorn and mix both with the batter while you warm about $^1/_2$ in (1.25 cm) of oil in a large pan.
3. Drop tablespoons of the mixture into the hot oil and cook for about 5 minutes, turning once.
4. Drain the fritters on kitchen roll and serve with burgers or chicken and salad, or with ketchup or a salsa dip.

BEAN BURGERS

The quantities given here make about 8 burgers. You don't need to be too precise with any of the ingredients and, if you don't have 5 Spice, season the burgers with curry powder, or just add mixed herbs, thyme, or Herbes de Provence.

For crisper burgers, deep fry in very hot oil instead of shallow frying.

1 tin of mixed beans
2 carrots
1 onion
1 tbsp flour (plain or gram)
2 tbsp breadcrumbs
1 tbsp red pesto
1 tsp 5 Spice
Oil

Method
1. Drain the tin of beans; rinse in a sieve under the cold tap then put them in a large bowl and break them up a bit with a potato masher.

2. Peel the onion, scrape the carrots and grate everything into the bowl with the beans.
3. Add the pesto to the bowl followed by the flour, breadcrumbs and seasoning and mix the whole lot together with a spoon.
4. Heat some oil in a frying pan while you make the mixture into patties with your hands.
5. Fry the burgers 4 or 5 at a time and cook for a couple of minutes on each side, keeping them warm in the oven as you go.
6. Serve inside mini pitta breads with any type of tomato sauce or yoghurt dressing, or with rice or couscous and salad.

SAUSAGES IN BBQ SAUCE

I've got no idea how the real thing is made, but this rough approximation of BBQ sauce tastes good to me …

This amount of sauce is enough to coat 8 large sausages or 12 chipolatas so double it up if you want more sauce to serve with the cooked sausages.

2 heaped tbsp tomato ketchup
1 tbsp vinegar
1 tbsp maple syrup

Method
1. Place sausages on an ovenproof tray, prick each one with a knife a few times and coat with the BBQ sauce.
2. Cook in the oven in the usual way; Gas Mark 6 (220ºC), for about half an hour.

SAUSAGES IN SPICY BBQ SAUCE

HP sauce is thinner and much tangier than tomato ketchup so the quantities are different, otherwise the general idea is exactly the same. And again, I can't claim that this tastes 100% authentic, but it's still good and takes only a few seconds to make, which makes it worth a try in my book.

1 heaped tbsp HP sauce
1 tbsp vinegar
2 tbsp maple syrup

Method
Coat sausages with the spicy BBQ sauce and cook in the usual way (see above).

PASTA

If there's a child anywhere on earth who doesn't like pasta I've yet to meet them, and it's a relief to know that no matter how desperate and short of time you are, you can always put pasta on a plate with tomato ketchup and grated cheese and call it dinner...

Tuna, pasta and sweetcorn is the next easiest, child-friendly pasta dish I know. (See also Pasta Soup, Chapter 2, 'Comfort Food'.)

TUNA, PASTA & SWEETCORN

For an even quicker option, just grate cheese (Cheddar or fresh Parmesan) over the food at the end, instead of making a cheese sauce.

Pasta shapes
1 large tin of tuna
Sweetcorn
1 oz (25 g) butter or margarine
1 tbsp of flour
1 mug or $^{1}/_{2}$ pint (300 ml) milk (approx)
1 oz (25 g) hard (Cheddar) cheese

Method

1. Cook the pasta in a pan of slightly salted boiling water according to the instructions on the packet, and add the drained tin of sweetcorn – or some frozen sweetcorn – for the last 2 minutes of the cooking time.
2. Meanwhile, make the cheese sauce by melting the butter or margarine in a saucepan and stirring in the flour to make a smooth paste. Cook over a low heat for a minute until the paste looks shiny and slips away from the bottom of the pan then add the milk and grated cheese, stirring or whisking all the time until the sauce thickens and is completely lump-free. (This only takes a few minutes.)
3. Drain the tinned tuna; strain the cooked pasta and sweetcorn and mix the two together.
4. Serve the tuna, pasta and sweetcorn in soup bowls or on dinner plates and pour the cheese sauce over the top.

Tip
Dried pasta is much more economical than fresh pasta (unless you've made it yourself) and, arguably, tastes better too.

PIZZA

You can't really go wrong with pizza, however you make it, so here are two very straightforward recipes that won't give you any trouble, either when you're making the pizza, or later on when you want your kids to eat it.

SUPER-QUICK-NO-WAIT PIZZA

Like the potato base pizza and pan pizza in Chapter 3, 'Loose Ends', there's no yeast involved here so it's ideal for making on busy school nights – or any day you simply don't have the time or the energy to make regular dough and wait for it to rise.

This makes one average 9–10 inch (23–25 cm) pizza but you could just as easily make two in the same amount of time, and although I've made this one cheese and tomato for the sake of simplicity, it goes without saying that, as with all pizza, you can use whatever you like for the topping.

4 rounded tbsp of self-raising flour (4 oz/100 g)
1 tsp baking powder
$^1/_2$ tsp salt
1 oz (25 g) grated cheese
1 egg
1 oz (25 g) melted butter
2 tbsp milk
Tomato purée
Garlic purée
Grated cheese
Tomatoes

Method

1. Sift the flour, baking powder and salt into a large mixing bowl with the grated cheese, stir well, then add the melted butter, milk and beaten egg.
2. Mix everything together with your hand and pinch the dough together into a soft ball.
3. Turn the dough out onto a floured surface and knead very gently for a minute or just long enough to make it smooth and ready to roll.
4. Roll the dough out to a rough circle and either press it into a well greased 9 inch (23 cm) cake tin or put it on an oiled baking tray. Fold the edge inwards, pressing gently into shape to make it neater.
5. Spread the dough with tomato and garlic purée, cover with the thinly sliced tomatoes and grated cheese and bake in the oven on Gas Mark 4–5 (180–190ºC) for 25–30 minutes, or until the pizza crust is crisp and golden and the cheese is bubbling.

PIZZA ROLLS

I thought of rolling up squares of uncooked pizza with the filling inside as a way of crisping the dough a bit more and making the end result less messy to eat with your hands.

When I've got the dough in the oven trays I normally mark it into the same number of pieces there'd be if I was going to cut the pizza up at the end but you can make bigger rolls than this if you feel like it, or even roll the pizza into pin-wheels and sprinkle the surfaces with grated mozzarella or Parmesan cheese for a bit of variation.

The quantities given below are enough to fill two large oven trays, which should give you at least six pieces of pizza each, and because the dough keeps so well in the fridge I sometimes make the pizzas up one at a time, saving half the amount of dough for another day.

For the pizza base
1 lb (550 g) plain flour
2 tsp (or 1 sachet) of dried yeast
1 tsp salt
1 tsp sugar
$^1/_2$ pint (275 ml) warm water mixed with 2 tsp oil
Tomato purée
Garlic purée

Suggested toppings
Cheese and tomato
Sausage and tomato
Gammon and pineapple
Tuna and sweetcorn
Prawns and tinned crab meat
Bolognese or Chilli sauce
Meatballs, peppers and onion
Spinach and ricotta
Mushroom and caramelized red onion
Mixed olives and green pesto

Method
1. Mix the dry ingredients together in a large bowl and make a well in the centre.
2. Pour the warm water and oil into the well and quickly mix everything together with your hand to make a soft dough. Turn the dough onto a floured surface and knead well for 5–10 minutes, sprinkling a little more flour whenever you feel you need to.

3. Place the dough in a greased bowl, cover with a damp tea towel and leave at the bottom of the oven on the lowest setting for about half an hour until the dough has almost doubled in size. (If you've got an airing cupboard you can prove the dough in there instead.)

4. Place the dough on a floured surface and knead again for another 5 minutes (known as 'knocking back') before covering with the damp cloth and proving for about half an hour – same as before – until the dough has doubled in size again.

5. Knock the dough back again and divide into two halves. (Keep one half in a food bag in the fridge if you don't want to use it straight away.)

6. Roll the dough out to fit the lightly oiled oven tray(s) – but not too thin unless you want the cooked dough to be really crisp – and press down well, folding any rough edges over and brushing the surface with a little more oil. Cover with cling film and keep in the fridge until you've got the topping ready.

7. Mark out the dough into six pieces then spread each piece with tomato purée, a little garlic purée and a couple of spoonfuls of topping, leaving about $^1/_4$ inch (5 mm) of edge all the way round.

8. Roll each piece of pizza up carefully with the sealed edge underneath.

9. Brush with a little olive oil and bake in the oven on Gas Mark 6 (200°C) for approximately 10 minutes until the dough is firm and just golden on the outside.

"Omit and substitute! That's how recipes should be written."

Jeff Smith

3
Loose ends

LEFTOVERS

———

I love the quote: "The most remarkable thing about my mother is that for thirty years she served the family nothing but leftovers. The original meal has never been found" (Calvin Trillin). And I also love leftovers, whether it's the remains of a curry reheated for lunch, or the last piece of birthday cake for breakfast.

The thing about leftovers is they tend to be a bit random, so don't expect too much from them and you won't be disappointed. Occasionally, you only need a couple of fresh ingredients to make one perfect meal roll over into a second equally perfect meal the next day, but far more often you'll find yourself cobbling the remains of two or three dinners together and adding salad or extra rice to make it stretch a bit further – which reminds me of 'leftover night' in the movie The Incredibles, *where each member of the family is eating something completely different for dinner …*

Anyway, it's a fact that plenty of foods actually taste better when they've been reheated, so unless you've got a very big dog, don't overlook your leftovers. Eat them all up and save yourself time, money, energy – and the hassle of even more supermarket shopping.

———

"If I've got at least a third of the ingredients in the recipe, I can make it."

Lukas Hyder

LEFTOVER CHICKEN PIE

The remains of about half a large chicken is perfect for this with cooked leftover sausages, potatoes, carrots and whatever else you can find; ham, bacon, mushrooms, spinach, peas or sweetcorn. The only thing that really matters is that there's lots of chunky stuff in the pie, as opposed to a few little bits and pieces floating around in a sea of gravy – which is what the so-called 'family pies' you find in the supermarket consist of.

Unless you're a keen and very experienced pastry maker (which is highly unlikely if you're reading this book) it's better – and much, much quicker – to use ready-made puff pastry, either fresh or frozen, than do it yourself.

1 lb (500 g) pack of ready-made puff pastry
Leftover cooked chicken
Leftover cooked sausages
Leftover cooked vegetables: potatoes, carrots, broccoli, cauliflower;
    also tinned peas, broad beans or sweetcorn
1 onion
Spinach
1 tin condensed soup (asparagus, mushroom or chicken)
Chicken stock
Milk
Oil
Salt & pepper

Method
1. Lightly grease the sides of a very large ovenproof dish (roughly 16 in x 10½ in/40 cm x 26 cm) with butter or margarine. Warm a little oil in a very large saucepan and fry the onion for

a couple of minutes before adding the chopped up chicken, sausages and leftover vegetables to the pan.

2. After a few minutes add the tin of condensed soup to the pan then fill the empty tin *twice* with milk or chicken stock, or a combination of the two, adding the extra liquid to the pan and giving it a good stir.

3. Add some fresh torn up spinach and/or a drained tin of sweetcorn to the pan, season with salt and pepper and keep over a very low heat while you roll out the pastry.

4. Roll out the whole packet of pastry until it looks about the right size to fit the dish, but try not to roll it out too large and too thin or you'll have a lot of waste and the layer of pastry on the pie won't be thick enough to puff up properly.

5. Put the filling into the dish then cover with the pastry, tucking the ends in around the edges *inside* the dish.

6. Brush the pastry with milk and bake the pie in the oven, Gas mark 6–7 (200–220ºC) for 15–20 minutes until the pastry is risen and golden.

7. Serve with any kind of potatoes, more vegetables or baked beans.

Tip

Leftover cooked chicken goes even further if you mince it. Minced chicken mixed with tarragon, salt, black pepper, a very little lemon juice and mayonnaise makes a great sandwich filling.

SWEET & SOUR CHICKEN

Leftover cooked chicken
1 red pepper
1 orange or yellow pepper
1 onion
1 standard tin of pineapple rings
2 tbsp (any) vinegar
2 tbsp tomato purée
2 tbsp soy sauce
1 rounded tbsp sugar (soft brown or white)
Oil
Plain flour

Method
1. Warm some oil in a large saucepan.
2. Cut the cooked chicken into rough pieces and coat in a little flour.
3. Fry the chicken on all sides for a couple of minutes; turn the heat right down and cover with a lid while you finely chop the onion and peppers then add them to the pan.
4. Cut 3 or 4 pineapple rings into small pieces and put them in with the vinegar, tomato purée, soy sauce, sugar and all the juice from the tin of pineapple.
5. Stir well, cover with a lid and simmer very gently for about 10 minutes.
6. Serve with rice.

> **Tip**
> Never throw a chicken carcass in the bin when all you
> have to do is immerse it in a saucepan of cold water and
> put it on the stove for a few hours to make great stock.
> Add a bay leaf or two, an onion cut into quarters and a
> couple of carrots (ditto) but if you don't have any of these
> to hand, just the chicken will do.

LEFTOVER CHILLI RECIPES

*Any kind of meaty sauce could be used for any of these recipes; I've only
specified chilli here because it's full of flavour, perfect for spicing up foods
with a milder taste, and it's the meal I tend to make in bulk most often.*

STUFFED MARROW

Marrow fell out of fashion years ago, not surprisingly, because on
its own and overcooked it's about as appetizing as a mouthful of
wet tissue.

But baked this way, when it's in season during the summer, the
softness and subtle flavour of the marrow contrasts nicely with the
taste and texture of the meat. (You could also stuff the marrow
with a mixture of chilli and cooked rice.)

1 medium–large marrow
Leftover chilli
   (*or* a mixture of leftover chilli and rice)
Butter
Salt & pepper

Method

1. Trim both ends of the marrow; cut the whole thing into rings approximately 2 in (5 cm) thick and scoop out the seeds from the middle of each ring to leave a fairly large, clean hole. (Leave the skin on even if you don't want to eat it; it helps the marrow keep its shape.)
2. Place the marrow rings in a large, lightly buttered Pyrex oven dish or casserole, sprinkle the marrow with salt and pepper then fill the holes and cover the top of each ring with the meat mixture.
3. Bake in a moderate oven, Gas Mark 4 (180°C) for about half an hour, or until the meat is piping hot and the marrow is soft but not collapsing.

Tip
Make Chilli Con Carne or Bolognese sauce stretch further by adding a couple of tins of chopped tomatoes and more seasoning.

CHILLI & TORTILLA CHIPS

Leftover chilli
2 large bags of tortilla chips
Grated mozzarella cheese
Avocado
Tomatoes (at least one per person)

Method

1. Reheat the chilli on Gas Mark 4 (180°C) in a large ovenproof dish covered with foil (or a lid) for about 20 minutes until the

food is piping hot. (Or reheat in the microwave before transferring to a large ovenproof dish.)

2. Empty both packets of tortilla chips over the chilli, mix them up a bit with the meaty sauce, then sprinkle liberally with grated cheese and return to the oven, or flash under the grill for a couple of minutes, so the cheese melts and the edges of the tortilla chips on the top brown ever so slightly. (Don't let them burn.)

3. Serve with chunks of avocado and tomato wedges.

> **Tips**
> Also use leftover chilli to stuff peppers and large beef tomatoes, or as a pizza topping or a filling for jacket potatoes or potato croquettes (see this chapter, 'Potatoes': Stuffed Potato Croquettes).
>
> Use up half-full jars of pesto in chilli (or Bolognese) as an alternative to sun-dried tomatoes.

LEFTOVER SAUSAGE RECIPES

QUORN SAUSAGE CHILLI

The obvious vegetarian alternative to any standard dish can be a bit boring and predictable sometimes, so instead of making chilli with vegetarian mince, try it with leftover Quorn sausages instead. If you've only got one veggie in your house you're likely to have these in the fridge quite often; if not, make the chilli with more sausages to begin with – and needless to say, this could also work well with real meaty sausages. (If you're using uncooked Quorn sausages, cook them in the pan a couple of minutes ahead of the vegetables.)

Leftover (cooked) Quorn sausages
Celery
Tomatoes
Mushrooms
Red pesto
Tomato Purée
Garlic Purée
2 tsp chilli powder
2 tsp cumin seeds
Oil
Water

Method
1. Slice the cold sausages, wash and chop the celery and mushrooms into chunks and roughly dice the tomatoes.
2. Warm a little oil in a large pan and fry the cumin seeds for a minute then add the sausages, celery and mushrooms and fry for a few minutes, turning the food over frequently to stop it sticking and burning.
3. Add the chilli powder to the pan followed by the tomatoes and a big spoonful of pesto and stir well before adding a generous amount of the tomato and garlic purées with a little water.
4. Stir well, adjust the consistency of the sauce with more water or tomato purée then cook for a few more minutes over a low heat until the food is hot. Serve with couscous or rice.

SAUSAGE & POTATO OMELETTE

This works best with cold new potatoes, or any potatoes with a waxy texture.

Eggs x 4 (or 1 per person)
Leftover cooked sausages
Leftover cooked potatoes
2 tomatoes
Parsley
Oil

Method
1. Warm some oil in a large frying pan while you cut the potatoes and sausages into small pieces.
2. Fry potatoes and sausages together for about 10 minutes until golden and crisping up on the outside then sprinkle with plenty of parsley.
3. Preheat the grill and thinly slice the tomatoes.
4. Beat the eggs together in a bowl with a splash of cold water then pour the eggs into the pan and whisk everything with a fork for a few seconds before turning the heat down under the pan. Put the sliced tomatoes in the omelette and leave it to set for a bit.
5. Finish cooking under the grill for a couple more minutes until the omelette is risen and golden.

Tips

Use uncooked spare sausages to make miniature meatballs by pushing the meat out of the skin and rolling into tiny balls with a little flour (or mix with leftover mince – ditto). Just add herbs and a couple of pinches of spice – curry powder, cumin, allspice and cayenne pepper are all good.

Make uncooked chipolatas into cocktail sausages by squeezing gently in the middle until you're down to the skin then twisting the two halves in opposite directions (so they look the way sausages normally do in a string) and separating with kitchen scissors.

LEFTOVER VEGETABLE RECIPES

BUBBLE & SQUEAK

Bubble & Squeak must be the most obvious leftover meal of all time but it's worth including simply because it's delicious, nutritious, and so easy to make it's a joke.

There are no rules really. Traditionally, bubble and squeak was made with leftover potatoes, cabbage and onions, but you can use whichever combination of vegetables you happen to have: broccoli, carrots, peas, swede, sweetcorn; it doesn't really matter. As long as you've got plenty of potatoes in there (and that includes sweet potato and butternut squash) anything goes.

Lots of leftover potatoes
Leftover vegetables
Oil or lard

Method
1. Mash all the leftover vegetables together and mix with the potatoes.
2. Preheat the oil or lard until it's practically smoking and fry the bubble and squeak in the biggest pan you've got. Alternatively, put it in a greased ovenproof dish, dotting the top all over with butter, and bake in a hot oven, Gas Mark 6–7 (200–220°C) until it's a deep golden brown all over the top.
3. If you're frying the bubble and squeak, keep turning it over in the pan with a vegetable slice or spatula so it browns nicely without sticking and burning.
4. Serve with sausages or bacon, baked beans and tinned tomatoes, or on its own with brown sauce or tomato ketchup.

(FISH WITH) ASPARAGUS SAUCE

I love fish, but unless it's deep-fried in batter or breadcrumbs it's a bit bland and boring without some kind of sauce to go with it.

You don't need the best-looking bit of the asparagus for this sauce, which is why it's perfect for using up the stalks and spring onions left over from the Asparagus Quiche recipe (Chapter 2, 'Cool Dinners') and needless to say, the same principle works equally well with unwanted broccoli stalks.

(If you have leftover boiled potatoes, cut them up into chunks and fry them once the sauce is simmering and the fish is cooking at Step 4.)

1 bundle of asparagus (minus the tips)
$^1/_2$ bundle of spring onions
$1^1/_2$ pints (850 ml) chicken or vegetable stock
2 tsp garlic purée
Small carton of single cream
Salt & pepper
Butter

Method

1. Roughly chop the asparagus. Finely chop the spring onions from one end to the other and set aside the dark green tops to sprinkle over the finished sauce at the end.
2. Warm some butter in a pan and fry the asparagus with the white part of the onions for a few minutes then add the stock and salt and pepper to taste.
3. Simmer for about 20 minutes until the asparagus is tender then purée in a blender or food processor with the garlic purée. (You can also add $^1/_2$ glass of white wine at this stage if you like.)
4. Meanwhile, poach, steam or bake some fresh salmon fillets or tuna steaks (and fry the potatoes).
5. Reheat the sauce with the single cream, adjust the seasoning, pour over the fish and top with the remainder of the spring onions.

STUFFED CABBAGE LEAVES

This is a good way of using up the largest outer leaves of large, dark green cabbages, so resist the temptation to discard them just because they're a bit muddy or ragged around the edges.

This is yet another recipe that would be good for a mixture of leftover Bolognese, chilli, or even chicken curry and rice, but here it's a vegetarian meal – although it could very easily be both at the same time if you've got meat to use up as well as the veggie ingredients.

8 large cabbage leaves
2 onions
Mushrooms
Small tin of sweetcorn
Leftover rice
2 tbsp pesto or curry paste
1 tin of chopped tomatoes
2 tbsp tomato purée
1 tsp basil
1 tsp mixed herbs or Herbes de Provence
Salt & pepper
Oil

Method

1. Wash the cabbage leaves and trim any very tough stalk ends; put in a pan of boiling water and simmer very gently for about 2 minutes then strain the water away and leave the cabbage leaves in the pan without a lid on until you need them.
2. Warm some oil in a large pan; fry the finely chopped onions and mushrooms until just soft then add the rice and cook for a few more minutes.
3. Drain the tin of sweetcorn and add to the pan with the pesto or curry paste and a spoonful or two of the chopped tomatoes if you think the mixture is a bit dry.
4. Wrap the mixture in the cabbage leaves and arrange the parcels in a large ovenproof dish.
5. Make a quick tomato sauce by boiling up the chopped tomatoes, tomato purée, salt and pepper and herbs in the same

pan you used to cook the vegetables.

6. Pour the tomato sauce over the cabbage parcels, cover with foil and bake in the oven on Gas Mark 4 (180ºC) for about half an hour, or until the filling is piping hot. Serve with lots of garlic bread.

> **Tip**
> A mixture of leftover cooked root vegetables – parsnips, turnips, swede, carrots – mixed with stock, or a mixture of stock and milk, can be made into a purée with a hand blender then layered with the meat and pasta instead of cheese sauce in a lasagne. (Sprinkle some grated cheese over the top.)

"Be eating one potato, peeling a second,
have a third in your fist and your eye on
a fourth."

Old Irish Proverb

POTATOES

Not only are potatoes packed with Vitamins B, B6 and C, as well as all the essential minerals, they're also fat-free, low in calories, an excellent carbohydrate, a good source of fibre (with their skins on) and contain no cholesterol. Never mind alfalfa sprouts and goji berries, potatoes are the original superfood – and if that's not enough to make you rush out and buy them in bulk, it's worth remembering that they're also dirt cheap – credit crunch or no credit crunch.

Lots of the supermarkets sell large sacks of potatoes (27 lb+/12.5 kg) for well under a fiver, and if you don't mind washing the dirt off (and why would you at that price?) you can't go wrong.

I love potatoes however they're cooked, and I can't think of any other food that's this versatile, nutritious, affordable and just plain perfect, which is why potatoes have got a section all to themselves in this book.

Tips
Don't keep potatoes in plastic bags. Unless they're in a brown paper sack to begin with, transfer them into an old cardboard box and store in a cool, dark, dry place.

Mixing mashed or diced fried potatoes with other vegetables makes the rest of the ingredients stretch further.

CHEESY POTATO BAKE

This is the same recipe as the Cheesy Potato Bake in Chapter 4, 'For Starters, Mains and Just Desserts'.

2 lb (1 kg) potatoes
Parmesan
Milk
Cheddar cheese
$^{1}/_{2}$ small (5 fl oz/150 ml) carton of single cream (optional)
Nutmeg
Salt & black pepper

Method
1. Wash, peel and thinly slice the potatoes.
2. Layer the potatoes with the grated cheese in a deep-sided casserole dish and sprinkle with nutmeg, salt and pepper. Start with potatoes and finish with cheese. (Grate more Cheddar on the top or use some fresh, grated Parmesan if you have it.)
3. Pour milk into the casserole dish to about halfway up the potatoes, adding $^{1}/_{2}$ a small carton of cream to the milk if you like.
4. Cover the casserole dish with foil, shiny side inwards, and bake in the oven on Gas Mark 3 (170°C) for about 1 hour.
5. Remove the foil, turn the oven up to Gas Mark 7 (220°C) and cook for another 20–30 minutes until the potatoes are soft all the way through and the topping is crisp and golden.

Tip
Make your own version of skimmed or semi-skimmed milk simply by adding cold water to whole milk; roughly half and half for skimmed milk and 1 part water to 2 parts milk for semi-skimmed. (*Eugh* is most people's reaction to this trick – but only if they know about it.)

CHEESY POTATO BREAD ROLLS

Even if the idea of baking bread like a perfect little housewife fills you with horror you must try these; they're completely delicious warm, cold or toasted. In fact, the lure of cheesy potato rolls filled with crispy bacon is enough to get the laziest teenager out of bed on a Saturday morning (all right then, Saturday afternoon) so make this bread on Friday evening and leave it to prove in the fridge overnight. That way you'll only have to knock the dough back once before shaping it into rolls and baking in the oven for about 15 minutes the next day.

A word of warning though; you must prove this dough cool, which is why leaving it in the fridge overnight is ideal. (If possible, use a large plastic food bag: put a spoonful of oil inside and rub the sides of the bag together. This leaves a thin film of oil on the inside surface of the bag, making it easier to get the dough out later on.) If you try and speed the process up by proving the dough in a warm place you'll be left with a gloopy mess that'll stick to everything and you won't even be able to get it off your hands, let alone into the oven. It doesn't matter if the potatoes and potato water are still warm when you're actually making the dough, though.

Finally, however good a recipe is, to my way of thinking the best ones have to have the simplicity factor, meaning you get a great result for the minimum amount of effort – and this is one of those recipes.

1½ lb + (800 g) strong bread flour
1 sachet dried yeast
4–6 medium-sized potatoes
½ pint (300 ml) potato water

1 tbsp natural yoghurt
1 tbsp salt
1–2 oz (25–50 g) stale hard cheese

Method

1. Peel and boil the potatoes in the usual way, then mash them and set the water aside to cool slightly while you get the rest of the ingredients ready.
2. Sift the flour into a very large bowl with the yeast and salt.
3. Make a well in the centre of the flour; add the mashed potatoes, potato water and yoghurt and mix it all together with your hand to form a soft, stickyish dough.
4. Turn the dough onto a floured surface and knead for a good 10 minutes, adding more flour as and when you need to.
5. Put the dough into a large food bag (or any suitably large container if you don't have food bags) and tie a knot in the bag at the very top so there's plenty of room for the dough to expand.
6. Leave in the fridge, preferably overnight, and when the dough has doubled in size preheat the oven to Gas Mark 6 (200ºC) and grease two large baking trays.
7. Turn the dough out onto a floured surface, knock it back and knead for a good ten minutes again, same as the first time, then tear the dough into satsuma-sized pieces, knead each piece separately for a minute and shape into rolls. Sprinkle with grated cheese, lightly pressing the cheese into the surface of the rolls.
8. Place the rolls on trays and bake near the top of the oven on Gas Mark 6 (200ºC) for 5–10 minutes then turn the oven down to Gas Mark 4 (180ºC) for another 5 minutes. When you tap the rolls underneath they should make a hollow sound, which means they're done.

> **Tip**
> Make skinny mash instead of peeling potatoes by washing them in cold water then boiling and mashing them in their skins. It saves time, you're not losing any of the vitamins and minerals in the water, and it's a lot nicer than it sounds.

HASH BROWNS

The quantities given below are enough for about 16 good-size hash browns.

2 lb (1 kg) potatoes
1 onion
3 tbsp butter, melted
3 tbsp flour (plain or wholemeal, or a mixture of each)

Method
1. Peel and grate the potatoes, wash them well in a colander to rinse away the starch, then squeeze dry in an old, clean tea towel.
2. Grate the onion and mix with the grated potatoes in a large bowl.
3. Sift the flour into the bowl, add the melted butter and mix the whole lot together.
4. Make the mixture into cakes with your hands and shallow fry in very hot oil for a few minutes on each side, flattening them out a bit with the vegetable slice.

To freeze the hash browns

1. If you want to freeze the hash browns, cook them first, drain on kitchen roll, layer them with greaseproof paper then place in a large food bag and freeze.
2. Reheat straight from the freezer by placing on an ovenproof tray and cooking in a hot oven, Gas Mark 7 (220°C) for 15–20 minutes.

Tip

If you buy potatoes in bulk, putting an apple in the bag with them – or two for a really big sack – can keep potatoes fresh for longer.

GNOCCHI

This is one recipe where you do need to cook the potatoes from scratch rather than using up cold mash from the fridge. It's easy enough to do, but you need fresh ingredients and a light touch to make a smooth, slightly sticky dough without overworking the mixture, otherwise the finished gnocchi will be too heavy. (You must use a floury variety of potato for the mash to be fine and completely lump-free.)

It's hard to be precise about the ratio of potatoes to flour but as a rough guide, I'd say 3–4 tablespoons of flour to 1 lb (500 g) of potatoes. Just be sure to add the flour a little at a time and you'll be able to tell when you've got the consistency you're after.

Have gnocchi with Bolognese and other meat or tomato-based sauces as a change from pasta, or with any kind of pesto, topped with grated Cheddar or Parmesan cheese.

2 lb (1 kg) potatoes
6 tbsp flour
Salt

Method
1. Don't peel the potatoes, give them a quick wash with a nail-brush in cold water and bring to the boil in a saucepan of cold water, simmering for about 20 minutes in the usual way until the potatoes are just soft.
2. Drain the potatoes and as soon as they're cool enough to handle, peel the skin off and put them in a large bowl. If you have a potato ricer press the potatoes through that, otherwise use a regular potato masher.
3. Beat the flour into the potatoes a little at a time and stop once the mixture is smooth and slightly sticky. Season with a little salt.
4. Cut the dough into quarters and roll each piece out on a floured surface into a long tube roughly the width of your finger. Cut the tubes into 1 in (2.5 cm)-long pieces, press your thumb into each piece and mark the other side with a fork to make a sort of shell.
5. Drop the gnocchi in batches into a very large pan of boiling water (don't overcrowd the pan) and wait for them to rise to the surface – this only takes a matter of seconds.
6. Once the gnocchi have risen, allow them to cook for another 10–15 seconds before removing from the pan with a slotted spoon and putting them in a bowl. Serve immediately with sauce or pesto while still warm.

POTATO BASE PIZZA

There's no getting away from pizza, and who would want to when it's so versatile, so easy to make, and such a big favourite with practically everyone ...

Potato-based pizza is one of my favourites because there's not much work in it and I think the results are as good as pizza made with a traditional dough base.

I've generalized a bit with the quantity of flour because it's hard to say on paper exactly how much you need, but start with 6 heaped tablespoons and if the dough still seems too sticky and doesn't come away from the sides of the bowl easily, add some more. (Even so, potato pizza dough is softer and more pliable than traditional dough, which is why it's important to bake it long enough to give it time to firm up properly.)

The quantities given here are perfect for an average-sized rectangular oven tray, approximately 15 x 10 in (37 x 25 cm).

1½ lb (600 g) potatoes
6–8 very heaped tbsp strong bread flour (plain will do if that's all you've got)
2 tbsp olive oil

Method
1. Peel, boil and mash potatoes in the usual way.
2. Put the potatoes into a large mixing bowl, sift in the flour and add 2 tbsp olive oil.
3. Mix everything together with your hand to form a firm, but still fairly soft, stickyish dough.
4. Grease the oven tray with a liberal amount of olive oil – more than you'd normally use if you were greasing the tray for baking

bread rolls, say.

5. Press the dough into the oven tray right up to the edges to make a smooth, even layer.

6. Cook the pizza base in a preheated oven, Gas Mark 6–7 (200–220ºC) for a good 20 minutes until the dough is crisp to the touch and golden brown all over.

7. Spread the pizza base with a mixture of 1 part garlic purée to 3 parts tomato purée; add your favourite toppings with lots of grated mozzarella (or a mixture of Cheddar and mozzarella) and bake in a hot oven (as above) for another 15–20 minutes.

POTATO SALAD

See also Chapter 2, 'Cool Dinners', for Classic Salads, salad dressings and the recipe for mayonnaise.

2 lb (1 kg) potatoes
3 spring onions
Mayonnaise
Natural yoghurt
Chives
Parsley
Lemon juice
Salt & pepper

Method

1. Wash and boil the potatoes in their skins until just soft, then leave to cool for a few minutes. (Either remove the skins while the potatoes are still warm, or leave them on.)

2. Dice the potatoes and put them in a large bowl with the mayonnaise (see page 111 for how to make it), yoghurt,

chopped spring onions, herbs, lemon juice and salt and pepper; mix gently and adjust the seasoning and consistency according to taste.

STUFFED POTATO CROQUETTES

These are hugely popular and easy to make in larger quantities than I've given here. You can also experiment with the fillings; I've even used leftover Bolognese before, and though I usually cook the potatoes fresh the same day, I don't see why this recipe couldn't work equally well with cold, leftover mash from the fridge.

As with all mashed potato recipes, the best kinds to use are the floury varieties.

2 lb (1 kg) – or roughly 4 medium-sized potatoes
2 tbsp cornflour
1 egg, beaten
1 tsp salt
Plain flour
Breadcrumbs
Oil

For the fillings
1 red onion
1 oz (25 g) feta cheese
2 oz (50 g) ham or leftover gammon
Mushrooms (6–8)

Method

1. Peel and mash the potatoes in the usual way (without milk or butter).

2. Mix the mashed potatoes, cornflour, beaten egg and salt together in a bowl to make a dough then turn out onto a floured surface (use plain flour for this) and knead gently for just a minute until it all comes together into a smooth, soft ball.

3. Wrap the dough in cling film and keep it in the fridge while you prepare the fillings.

4. Warm some oil in a large frying pan while you finely chop the red onion, mushroom and ham (or gammon) then put the onions in and cook for a few minutes before moving them over to one side of the pan and frying the mushrooms. (Cook them separately if you prefer, but I don't see the point of getting more than one pan dirty when it doesn't matter if you get a bit of crossover between the two ingredients.)

5. Put the mushrooms in one bowl with the chopped ham and the red onion in another bowl with the roughly crumbled feta cheese. Spread a few ounces of breadcrumbs out on a dinner plate.

6. Divide the dough into quarters and mark each quarter into 3 to make 12 pieces of dough. (You may want to make the pieces a bit bigger, in which case you should still comfortably get 10 croquettes.)

7. Wet your hands with cold water and form each piece of dough into a patty with the palms of your hands. Don't be tempted to use flour for this bit – and don't worry about the dough being soft either, it's very easy to squish into shape around the filling.

8. Holding the patty on the palm of one hand, put a couple of teaspoons of filling in the middle and fold the dough around

the filling, patting it gently into a sort of rounded oval shape.
9. Lightly roll each croquette in the breadcrumbs and shallow fry in about 1 inch (2.5 cm) of oil before finishing them off in the oven for another 10 minutes on Gas mark 5–6 (190–200°C), or for a minute or two in the microwave.
10. Serve warm with salad, or cold meat and salad.

VEGETARIAN MOUSSAKA

1 lb (500 g) potatoes
1 aubergine
2 courgettes
2 red onions
2 cloves of garlic
1 tin of chopped tomatoes
2 tbsp tomato purée
4 oz (100 g) feta cheese
1 tub of Greek yoghurt or crème fraîche
1 (large) egg
1 tsp sugar
$^1\!/_2$ tsp salt
Herbes de Provence
Parmesan cheese
Olive oil

Method
1. Slice the aubergine and courgettes then put them in a bowl and sprinkle with lots of salt. Leave for about half an hour then rinse well in cold water and drain.
2. Put the potatoes into a pan of boiling water and simmer for a few minutes then remove the pan from the heat, strain the

water off and leave the potatoes to cool for a bit.

3. Peel and slice the red onions and as soon as the potatoes are cool enough to handle, peel and slice them thinly then mix with the aubergine, courgettes and onion on a large oiled baking tray. Drizzle with olive oil and bake in a preheated oven, Gas Mark 7 (220ºC) for about 15 minutes.

4. Meanwhile, warm more olive oil in a large pan. Fry the crushed garlic then add the chopped tomatoes, tomato purée, sugar, salt and herbs and bring to the boil. Simmer for 5 minutes, stirring continuously as the sauce thickens.

5. Put roughly half the roasted vegetables in a large ovenproof dish and pour over half the tomato sauce. Crumble the feta cheese over the tomato sauce then cover with the remainder of the vegetables followed by the rest of the tomato sauce.

6. Mix the yoghurt or crème fraîche with the beaten egg and some finely grated Parmesan cheese, spread the topping over the moussaka and finish with more grated cheese.

7. Bake the moussaka in the oven, still at Gas Mark 7 (220ºC), for 20–25 minutes until the topping is very brown and bubbly. Serve with salad or green vegetables.

FISHCAKES

Although fish is obviously the main ingredient, as far as I know all fishcakes are made with potatoes or something very similar (i.e. sweet potatoes or butternut squash), which is why they're here in the potato section.

In fact, not only are fishcakes a real convenience food however you make them, they seem to appeal to almost everyone, including your average fussy little eater (especially with chips) so here are a few of my favourites, starting with the most basic and working up to the (slightly) more sophisticated. (See also the Squash and Salmon Fishcakes recipe in Chapter 4.)

QUICK BAKED FISHCAKES

If you haven't got leftover mashed potatoes use instant mash instead. (The fishcakes can also be kept in the fridge after cooking and reheated in the microwave.)

Makes about 8

1 tin of tuna, any size
1 tin of sweetcorn, any size
2 eggs, beaten
Leftover mash (roughly 1 lb/500 g potatoes)
    or
1 packet of instant (made up according to the instructions on the packet)
Salt & pepper

Method

1. Grease a large oven tray and preheat the oven to Gas Mark 6 (220°C)
2. Put leftover mash in a large bowl or make up the instant mash according to the instructions on the packet.
3. Drain the tins of tuna and sweetcorn and mix up in the bowl with the potatoes and beaten egg. Season.
4. Put big spoonfuls of the fish cake mixture on the oven tray and shape roughly into rounds with a fork.
5. Bake in the oven for about 20 minutes until the outside is firm and golden.

PRAWN & WHITE FISHCAKES

Makes about 12
4 fairly large potatoes
6 small frozen skinless white fish fillets
   or
1 large fresh white fish fillet (e.g. pollack)
1 small packet of frozen prawns
Lemon juice
Butter
Milk
Black pepper
Breadcrumbs

Method
1. Defrost the prawns and cook the white fish in an ovenproof dish according to the instructions on the packet, or for about 15 minutes for fresh fish.
2. Meanwhile, boil the potatoes with or without the skins before mashing them with a tablespoonful of butter and some milk.
3. Put the fish in a mixing bowl and flake with a fork, then add the defrosted prawns and season with lots of lemon juice and black pepper.
4. Combine the contents of the bowl with the mashed potatoes and form the mixture into fishcakes with your hands.
5. Gently press the fishcakes into a tray of breadcrumbs on both sides and fry in a large pan for a few minutes, turning once. Put the fishcakes in the oven at Gas Mark 5 (190ºC) to warm through, and serve with chips or potato wedges and green vegetables or salad.

FRESH MACKEREL FISHCAKES WITH LEMON & ROQUEFORT

You could use smoked mackerel for these, but fresh is no more expensive and because it's less salty I think the flavours of the lemon and cheese come through better.

Makes 10–12 fishcakes
2 lb (1 kg) potatoes
4 fresh mackerel fillets
1 lemon
1½ oz (40 g) Roquefort cheese
Butter
Black pepper
Breadcrumbs
Oil

Method
1. Peel, boil and mash the potatoes in a large bowl with a little butter then add the crumbled cheese and the finely grated rind of the lemon, plus all the juice. Season with black pepper.
2. Put the fish in a casserole dish with the remains of the lemon and just enough water to cover the fish, and poach in the oven on Gas Mark 5 (190°C) for about 15 minutes, until the fish is tender.
3. Spread some breadcrumbs on a large dinner plate and warm about 1 in (2 cm) of oil in a large pan.
4. Meanwhile, remove the skin of the mackerel and flake the fish carefully to check for any bones, then thoroughly mix the mackerel with the other ingredients and shape into cakes with your hands.

5. Coat the fishcakes in the breadcrumbs and fry for a few minutes until golden, turning once; then finish the fishcakes off in the oven on Gas Mark 5 (190°C). Serve with grilled tomatoes and rice.

BAKED POTATO FISHCAKES

You could use tinned fish or a combination of tinned and fresh, but I like making these with fresh white fish fillets that have just been broken up a bit and stirred into the potato, rather than thoroughly mashed and mixed in completely.

One small-to-medium piece of fish is enough for two very large baking potatoes, making four halves. (Mix the potato with a ready-made soft cream cheese with herbs and garlic instead of making garlic butter if you prefer.)

2 very large baking potatoes
1 white fish fillet
1 oz (25 g) grated Cheddar
1 tbsp butter
2 cloves of garlic
2 tsp chives or parsley
Salt & pepper

Method
1. Wash the potatoes and prick several times with a sharp knife before putting in the microwave on full power for 10 minutes then wrapping in foil and baking in the oven, Gas Mark 5 (190°C) for about half an hour.
2. Meanwhile, poach the fish in boiling water (or a combination

of water and milk) for 10–15 minutes.

3. Transfer the fish to a bowl, remove the skin and check for bones, then flake the fish with a fork.

4. Mash the butter with a fork and mix with the crushed garlic and herbs.

5. Once the potatoes are cooked and cool enough to handle, cut them in half, scoop out the insides (but not so much that the skins fall apart) and mash with the garlic butter and a very little milk.

6. Combine the flaked fish with the mashed potato and season with salt and pepper before piling the mixture back into the potato skins and topping with grated cheese.

7. Bake in the hottest part of the oven for about 10 minutes, or until the cheese is melted and golden and the potatoes are hot right the way through.

Tips

Leftover rice gives a nice texture to some fishcake mixtures, especially if mixed with finely chopped peppers, sweetcorn and other bits and pieces.

Fishcakes hold their shape much better if they're coated in breadcrumbs, especially when frying or grilling, but I don't see the point of dipping in flour and beaten egg first when all that does is waste time (and eggs) and make a mess. (Whenever you're frying *anything* that breadcrumbs will stick to without any help, it makes sense to leave out the flour and beaten eggs.)

"Why bother to cook TV dinners? I suck them frozen."

Woody Allen

TAKE ONE

However daunting it may seem sometimes, making big dinners for the whole family is often easier than trying to cook for one – unless you make twice as much as you need each time and eat the leftovers the next night – so it's handy to have a few ideas for shortcut meals and scaled down dinners for those days when you find yourself cooking for one, or maybe two people, whatever the reason.

LEMON & LIME FISH BAKE

Fresh fish just needs a quick rinse in cold water, but if you're using frozen fish, defrost it in the microwave first. (Fish fillets frozen into blocks with the skin removed will need to be precooked according to the instructions on the packaging.)

If you want to make this for more than two people, use more fish but don't try and water the soup down to make it go further; there should still be enough sauce for at least four people.

1 large fish fillet (per person)
1 tin of Campbell's condensed Cream of Asparagus soup
Milk or water
1 leek
Mushrooms
Lemon juice
Lime juice
Parsley
Salt & pepper
1 tbsp butter

Method

1. Wash and prepare the fish and place in a large casserole dish. (If you're cooking more, it doesn't matter if the fillets overlap each other.)
2. Wash and slice the leeks and mushrooms, warm the butter in a pan and fry the vegetables for a few minutes until the leeks are just soft.
3. Add the tin of soup to the pan, then half-fill the tin with milk, rinse out and add to the pan, stirring for another minute.
4. Add lemon juice and lime juice to the pan according to taste and pour the sauce over the fish.
5. Sprinkle with parsley, season with salt and pepper and bake in a moderate oven, Gas Mark 4 (180ºC) for about 20 minutes.

Tip

Buy pre-packed fresh vegetable assortments in the supermarket. This wouldn't normally work for a family but it's an affordable option for one or two people and a good way of reducing, or avoiding, waste altogether.

PAN PIZZA

This is very similar to the potato base pizza in Chapter 3, 'Potatoes', made even easier by the fact that you only have to whisk an egg and some flour into half a packet of instant mash instead of cooking fresh potatoes, but this dough is much looser so you'll probably find you have to eat the pizza with a knife and fork rather than picking it up with your hands.

Although it's a recipe for one it needs to be cooked in a fairly large pan and you may still find there's enough for two people, depending on the amount of topping you put on the pizza and how hungry you are ...

(For suggested pizza toppings see the Pizza section in Chapter 2, 'Kids' Favourites'.)

$^1/_2$ packet (5 oz /142 g) instant mashed potato
1 egg
$1^1/_2$ tbsp plain flour
(Milk)
1 cup of boiling water
Oil
Tomato purée
Garlic purée

Toppings
Grated cheese

Method
1. Empty roughly half a packet of instant mashed potato into a bowl, pour on the boiling water and whisk vigorously with a fork, adding the egg and sifted flour to make a thick paste. (The potato mixture needs to be quite stiff but if it feels too dry whisk in a little cold milk to get the right consistency.)
2. Warm some oil in a large frying pan and once it's hot put the potato mixture in and smooth it across the bottom of the pan in an even layer.
3. Cook over a low heat for about 5 minutes while you preheat the grill then put the pan under the grill and cook for another 5 minutes, or until the top is lightly browned.
4. Use the back of a tablespoon to spread the potato base with

tomato and garlic purée, then add your topping, sprinkle with lots of grated cheese and finish cooking the pizza under the grill until the topping is hot and the cheese is bubbling.

> **Tip**
> Buy individually wrapped value range pizzas from the supermarket and customize them with ham and pineapple, sliced sausages and red pesto, leftover Bolognese or chilli sauce, tuna and sweetcorn, tomatoes and extra cheese ...

RAREBIT

There are quite a few variations of rarebit, which is basically a well-flavoured cheesy sauce on toast. Other than that I'm not sure exactly what the variations are, what they're called or where they originate from. I only have a rough idea of what a rarebit recipe consists of, and the various ways you could make it at home.

The quantities in each of these recipes will be enough for (at least) two slices of toast.

For the sauce
1 oz (25 g) butter or margarine
1 oz (25 g) flour
1 mug of milk
1 egg yolk
$1/2$ oz (15 g) Cheddar cheese
1 tsp Dijon or English mustard
Salt & pepper

Method

1. Melt the butter in a small saucepan, remove from the heat for a minute while you stir in the flour then cook for another minute until the paste is shiny and slipping away from the bottom of the pan.
2. Add the milk gradually, stirring all the time with a wooden spoon (or use a small hand whisk), and cook for a few minutes until you have a smooth sauce.
3. Stir in the beaten egg yolk, cheese and mustard and season with salt and pepper according to taste.

1. **Cheese and Onion Rarebit:** Finely chop half an onion then melt a bit more butter or margarine in a small saucepan than specified in the list of ingredients (say 1¹⁄₂ oz (40 g) instead of just 1 oz (25 g)) and cook the onion before adding the flour. Alternatively, fry the onion separately in a little more butter or oil, or poach it in a mugful of stock and add to the sauce at the end.
2. **Cheese, Ham and Onion Rarebit:** Same as above, with one or two slices of ham (with extra mustard if you like) on each piece of toast. Cover the ham with the cheese and onion sauce.
3. **Poached Egg Rarebit:** Make the sauce in the usual way then poach one egg per piece of toast in slightly salted boiling water for a few minutes. Cover the egg with the sauce and season with black pepper.
4. **Egg and Spinach Rarebit:** Otherwise known as Oeuf Florentine. Instead of toast, cook a couple of handfuls of fresh spinach in the microwave with a very little water then drain well and serve with soft poached eggs and the sauce poured over the top.
5. **Tomato and Cheese Rarebit:** Make the sauce in the usual way. Toast the bread on one side; turn it over and cover the

uncooked side with thinly sliced tomato seasoned with salt and pepper. Put back under the grill until the tomatoes are as brown as they can be without the toast underneath actually igniting; serve with the sauce poured over the top.

6. **Tuna and Cheese Rarebit:** Brilliant for using up the remains of a tin of tuna if you've used the first half to make a sandwich. Toast the bread on one side; turn it over and spread the uncooked side with the tuna. Put back under the grill just long enough to take the chill off the tuna (assuming it's been in the fridge) and serve with the sauce poured over the top.

Tip
Make almost-instant soup with packets of mixed fresh vegetables. Just cook them in stock and seasoning, add milk, cream, wine or whatever you fancy and blend in a food processor.

CREAMED MUSHROOMS

This makes an ideal filling for jacket potatoes; or serve it with rice, couscous or quinoa.

Button mushrooms
1 small onion
1 small carton of single cream
2 tsp cornflour
2 tsp curry paste
Lemon juice
Parsley

Salt & black pepper
Butter

Method

1. Melt the butter in a pan and fry the finely chopped onion for a couple of minutes until it starts to soften, then add the sliced (or halved) mushrooms.
2. Sift in the cornflour and quickly stir it in; cook for a couple of minutes then slowly pour the cream into the pan, still stirring.
3. Once the sauce is thickening add the curry paste; stir again then simmer very gently for a few more minutes.
4. Add lemon juice according to taste then season with salt and pepper, sprinkle with parsley and serve.

Tip

Make quick and easy sauces in small quantities:

(a) 1 small tub of crème fraîche and a couple of handfuls of grated cheese;
(b) 1–2 tbsp of flour or cornflour sifted and stirred into a pan of fried onion and mushrooms, followed by $^1/_4$ pint (150 ml) of stock or 1 small bottle of cider, or a glass of wine.

HOT LAMB CHOPS

Make with lamb chops or cutlets.

Lamb chops or cutlets
$^1/_4$ pint (150 ml) of water
2 tbsp tomato ketchup
1 tbsp wine or cider vinegar

1 tbsp Worcestershire sauce
Tabasco sauce
2 tsp soft brown sugar
1 tsp salt
1 tsp chilli powder

Method
1. Mix ¹/₄ pint (150 ml) of cold water with the tomato ketchup, vinegar, Worcestershire sauce, sugar, salt and chilli powder, whisking everything together with a fork until well blended.
2. Add a few drops of Tabasco sauce – or a good shake, depending on how hot you want it – and pour the marinade into a large dish.
3. Put the chops or cutlets in the marinade, turning them over to coat them as much as you can, then cover and leave in the fridge for 2–3 hours.
4. Preheat the grill, put the lamb on the rack and brush with more marinade then cook for 5–10 minutes on each side, according to the size and thickness of the meat. (Baste the meat with marinade again when you turn the lamb over.)
5. Serve with rice, couscous or noodles and salad, or with mashed potatoes and green vegetables.

Tip
Jacket potatoes, baked sweet potatoes, pasta bakes and noodles are all easy meals to cook for just one or two people without making leftovers.

Also try ...
Fish Finger Pie (Chapter 2, 'Kids' Favourites');
Sausages in BBQ Sauce (Chapter 2, 'Kids' Favourites');
Stuffed Potato Croquettes (Chapter 3, 'Loose Ends: Potatoes');
Potato Skins (Chapter 4, 'For Starters ...');
Chicken Liver Pâté (Chapter 4, 'For Starters ...');
Squash & Salmon Fishcakes (Chapter 4, 'Mains ...');
Egg & Bacon Salad (Chapter 4, 'For Starters ...');
Baked Fish in Horseradish Sauce (Chapter 4, 'Mains ...');
Chicken Kiev and Chicken Cordon Bleu (Chapter 2, 'Classics');
Pacific Pie (Chapter 2, 'Classics').

"The golden rule when reading the menu in a
restaurant is, if you can't pronounce it,
you can't afford it."

Frank Muir

4
For starters, mains and just desserts

It may seem strange to have a chapter of dinner party menus in an everyday low-cost family cookbook, but it still holds true that you can make a three-course meal for four or five people at home for about the same amount of money you'd spend on a single main course in a mid price range restaurant, and that seems like a good enough reason for a dinner party to me.

Most, if not all, of these recipes are as simple and affordable as everything else in the book, and lots of them would make a good stand-alone dinner on an ordinary week night too. In fact, plenty of restaurant menus only give the impression that the food's a bit special because of the totally over-the-top descriptive style they're written in; i.e. everything's smothered in this, encrusted in that, or nestling on a bed of something, or it's been 'stone-baked' or 'pan-fried' … as if anyone ever fries anything without using a pan.

Anyway, look closely at your average restaurant menu and you'll probably find the vast majority of the dishes on offer are well within your capabilities. The same applies here, only more so.

NETTLE SOUP

SQUASH & SALMON FISHCAKES

SWEETLOAF

NETTLE SOUP

If you think your guests will be completely turned off by the thought of eating stinging nettles, tell them this is watercress. The two are so similar they'll probably be none the wiser. Just remember you can't use sprigs of fresh nettle as a garnish, and wear your rubber gloves for the first part, the nettles don't lose their sting till they're cooked.

Obviously you really can make the soup with watercress instead, but it's always good to try something a bit different and nettles cost nothing so give them a go ...

Nettles (the equivalent of an average bag of watercress)
1 onion
2 cloves of garlic
1 pint (600 ml) chicken stock
$^1/_4$ pint (150 ml) milk
2 heaped tbsp plain flour
2 tsp dried parsley
1tsp nutmeg
Butter
Salt & pepper
Vinegar

Method

1. Wearing your rubber gloves, pick the youngest, bright green, nettles you can find (after all, they're *everywhere*), about 6–8 in (15–20 cm) from the top.
2. Wash the nettles thoroughly in a big bowl of salty water and rinse them under the cold tap to be sure they're clean.
3. Warm some butter in a large saucepan while you peel and roughly chop the onion and crush the garlic, then put both in the pan together and cook gently for a few minutes until the onion has softened.
4. Squeeze excess water from the nettles – still wearing the rubber gloves – and add them to the pan with a teaspoonful of vinegar. Cover the pan with a lid and simmer gently for about 5 minutes before adding the chicken stock, milk and nutmeg.
5. Stir well and bring the soup to the boil; meanwhile put 2 heaped tablespoons of plain flour, 1 tablespoon of butter and a couple of teaspoons of dried parsley in a cup or small bowl and mash together till smooth.
6. As soon as the soup has started to boil, turn the heat right down and add the parsley, butter and flour mixture, stir until dissolved then leave to simmer gently for about 5 minutes.
7. Blend the soup, and if you want it thicker, whisk in a couple of spoonfuls of instant mash.

SQUASH & SALMON FISHCAKES WITH LEMON & MUSTARD MAYO

One large butternut squash and two salmon fillets make about a dozen fishcakes. One fishcake served with the dressing and a salad garnish makes a good starter, but for the main course, as they are here, you'll want two fishcakes per person, so increase the mixture whichever way you like – using extra salmon or adding a sweet potato to the baked squash – if you want to make more than 12.

1 butternut squash
2 fresh salmon fillets (or more)
2 eggs, beaten with a splash of milk
2 tbsp flour
Chives
Lemon juice
Salt & pepper
Olive oil
Mayonnaise
English mustard
Butter

Method

1. Preheat the oven to Gas Mark 5 (190°C). Peel the butternut squash, cut into small chunks, drizzle with olive oil and roast in the oven for about 20 minutes.
2. At the same time, put the salmon fillets in a small casserole dish with a lid and bake at the bottom of the oven. (Check after 15 minutes; if the fish is already cooked through, take it out.)
3. Mash the squash in a large bowl with some butter, season with salt and pepper and add the flaked fish, chives, and a splash of lemon juice.
4. Sift 2 tbsp flour into the mixture and blend everything together.
5. Beat the eggs and milk in a small bowl and warm more olive oil in a frying pan.
6. Pick up ice-cream-scoop-sized portions of fishcake mixture and shape into small oval patties with your hands, keeping the handling to a minimum.

7. Dunk the fishcakes in the egg mixture, flipping over once, then pop them straight into the pan – little pools of egg will form around the fishcakes in the pan – and cook for a few minutes on each side, turning once.
8. Make the lemon and mustard mayo by blending approximately 4 tablespoons of mayonnaise with 1 teaspoon each of mustard and lemon juice according to taste. (Make double this amount if you like.)
9. Serve the fishcakes with potato wedges or oven chips and salad, with a spoonful of the mayo on the side.

SWEETLOAF

I've said rich tea or malted milk biscuits in the list of ingredients, but loads of other biscuits work well with this recipe: KitKats, Viscount biscuits, Penguins, digestives or stale ginger nuts.

You can also add chopped hazelnuts and glacé cherries.

1½ lb (1 kg) milk chocolate
or
half milk, half plain chocolate
4 oz (100 g) unsalted butter
8 rich tea or malted milk biscuits
A generous handful each of mini marshmallows and raisins

Method
1. *Very lightly* grease and long-strip line a standard size (1 lb) loaf tin.
2. Break the chocolate into small pieces and put it in a bowl over a pan of boiling water to melt.
3. Melt the butter separately – in the microwave is good; about 40

seconds on defrost – and don't be tempted to try and melt the butter and chocolate together, it doesn't work.

4. Wash and dry the raisins, break up the biscuits on a dinner plate or in a bowl; add the dried fruit and marshmallows and mix it all together.

5. When the chocolate has melted stir in the melted butter followed by the rest of the ingredients and pour the mixture into the lined loaf tin,

6. Leave to chill in the fridge for several hours – preferably overnight – cut into wafer thin slices and serve. The colder the chocolate, the easier it is to cut into slithers, but if you don't have time to chill overnight you can always cut the sweetloaf into thick slices, then cut the slices into fingers.

DEEP-FRIED CAMEMBERT

BEEF IN BEER

CHOCOLATE MOUSSE

DEEP-FRIED CAMEMBERT WITH CRANBERRY SAUCE

Camembert may not be the cheapest cheese on the block but if you already have flour, oil and sesame seeds in the cupboard and breadcrumbs in the freezer, this starter won't make that much of a dent in the budget – and it's quite heavy so you'll only need one portion of cheese per person. (Make sure the cheese has been kept cool in the fridge for a few hours first.)

Cranberry sauce can be made by stewing fresh cranberries in a pan with plenty of sugar and a very little water; add a couple of teaspoons of cinnamon or a mixture of cinnamon and ginger and let the fruit simmer for about 20 minutes, then leave to stand in the pan for a couple of hours till the sauce thickens and goes all jammy, adding more sugar – or golden syrup – at the end if you think you need it. (Or use maple syrup – or give the sauce a bit more zing with half a glass of sherry or brandy.) If cranberries are in season, chances are they'll also be on special offer – not that they're necessarily expensive – but if they're not in season or you don't want to make your own, use ready-made cranberry sauce or redcurrant jelly, or a jar of baby apple purée instead.

1 individually wrapped portion of Camembert per person
Breadcrumbs (approximately 4 oz/100 g = 4 slices of bread)
Sesame seeds (say 2 tbsp)
2 tbsp flour
1 egg and a splash of milk
Oil for deep-frying

Method
1. Fill 3 small bowls: 1 with the flour, 1 with the beaten egg and milk, 1 with the breadcrumbs and sesame seeds mixed together.
2. Dust each portion of cheese with a little flour before dipping into the beaten egg mixture and coating with the breadcrumbs and sesame seeds.
3. Keep the prepared cheese portions in the fridge until the last minute. If they're not properly chilled the cheese will ooze and run in the pan.
4. Heat enough oil in a deep-sided pan to just cover the cheese portions. (Test the temperature by dropping a small chunk of bread into the oil; if it's hot enough the bread will turn golden

brown in a matter of seconds.)

5. Fry the cheese portions for 2–4 minutes, drain on kitchen roll and serve warm with cranberry sauce or apple purée.

BEEF IN BEER WITH CHEESY POTATO BAKE & GREEN VEGETABLES

As with most of the other recipes in this book, you don't have to worry about exact quantities, especially with the meat, and you really only need one bottle of beer, but it's a good idea to have an extra bottle on standby so if you find your casserole drying out near the end of the cooking time you can just add more. If you run out of beer, add more beef stock. And if, like me, you don't know the difference between brown ale and bitter – or are they the same thing? – look for the words lager or pale ale somewhere on the label and you won't go far wrong.

Although the method is short and straightforward the cooking time is quite long so you'll have to make this in advance unless you've got the whole afternoon. In fact, keeping any sauce-based dish in the fridge for a few hours – or even a couple of days – is a great way to concentrate the flavours, so it pays to make this casserole long before you need it in any case.

Serves 4–6
2 lb+ (1.5 kg) stewing steak
$^{1}/_{2}$ lb (225 g) back bacon
1 large or 2 medium onions
1 or 2 cloves of garlic

3 tbsp flour
$^1/_2$ pint (300 ml) beef stock (1 stock cube)
2 tbsp vinegar
2 tsp sugar (preferably brown)
$^1/_2$ tsp nutmeg
Oil or lard
Salt & pepper
Small French stick
Mustard (English, French or Dijon)
1–2 bottles of beer

Method
1. Warm the fat or oil in a large pan while you trim any excess fat off the meat (stewing steak and bacon). Season with a little salt and pepper if you like.
2. Fry the onions and garlic on high for a couple of minutes till slightly golden then add all the meat to the pan and brown quickly on all sides.
3. Sift the flour into the pan and stir well to coat the meat.
4. Turn the heat right down for a minute – or take the pan off the hob altogether to stop the meat sticking – while you make up the stock.
5. Mix the beef stock, beer, vinegar, sugar and nutmeg together in a large measuring jug and pour slowly into the pan with the meat, stirring constantly for a couple of minutes until the gravy thickens slightly.
6. Transfer everything from the pan into a very large casserole dish with a lid and cook in a very low oven, approximately Gas Mark 2 (160ºC), or even lower if you have a fan oven, for about two hours.
7. Skim any fat from the top of the casserole and check that the beef is tender.

8. Thinly slice into rings enough French bread to cover the top of the casserole, spread one side of each piece of bread with mustard and layer the bread, mustard side down, across the top of the casserole.
9. Turn the oven up to Gas Mark 6 (200°C) and cook for another 20–30 minutes until the bread is crisp and golden.

CHEESY POTATO BAKE

If you're making the beef in beer from scratch on the night, put the Cheesy Potato Bake in the oven once the beef has been cooking for an hour. If you're reheating the beef, the potato bake will need to go in at the same time.

Potatoes (at least 1 large per person)
Cheddar cheese
Parmesan
Milk
½ small carton of single cream
Nutmeg
Salt & pepper

Method
1. Wash, peel and thinly slice as many potatoes as you think you need for the number of people you're feeding, and if in doubt do too much; leftover Cheesy Potato Bake can be reheated in the microwave later on.
2. Layer the potatoes with grated cheese and a sprinkling of nutmeg and seasoning in a deep-sided casserole dish, starting with potatoes and finishing with a topping of cheese. (Use more Cheddar or fresh, grated Parmesan if you have it.)

3. Pour milk into the casserole dish to about halfway up the potatoes and don't swamp it. (Add $\frac{1}{2}$ a small carton of cream to the milk if you like.)

4. Cover the casserole dish with foil, shiny side inwards, and bake in the oven on Gas Mark 3 (160°C) for about 1 hour.

5. Remove the foil, turn the oven up to Gas Mark 6 (220°C) and cook for another 20–30 minutes until the topping is crisp and golden. If the potatoes aren't quite soft enough by the time the beef is ready, remove the beef from the oven and keep warm on the top then cover the potatoes with the foil again, turn the oven up to the highest setting and cook for another 10 minutes.

6. Approximately 10 minutes before the end of the cooking time steam or simmer fresh broccoli, French beans, Savoy cabbage or spring greens.

CHOCOLATE MOUSSE

This chocolate mousse is as easy as it gets, but because it needs to be chilled for a couple of hours you could make this the night before too.

Serves 4–6
8 oz (225 g) plain chocolate
4 eggs
1 tbsp instant coffee dissolved in 4 tbsp boiling water
1 tbsp sherry or brandy
1 level tbsp icing sugar

Method

1. Dissolve the coffee in the boiling water.
2. Break the chocolate into pieces and melt in a bowl over a saucepan of boiling water with the coffee and sherry, stirring occasionally while you separate the eggs.
3. Once the chocolate mixture is completely smooth remove from the heat and leave to cool for a minute before you beat the egg yolks into the mixture.
4. Whisk the egg whites in a separate bowl until stiff; add the icing sugar then whisk for another minute until stiff enough to stand up in peaks.
5. Fold the beaten egg whites into the chocolate mixture and spoon into small glass bowls or ramekins.
6. Chill for at least 3 hours then dust with icing sugar (mixed with cocoa powder if you've got it) and serve with thick cream.

CHICKEN LIVER PÂTÉ

BEEF STROGANOFF

ORANGES IN CARAMEL

CHICKEN LIVER PÂTÉ

Another good one for making well in advance and leaving in the fridge till you need it. Add a teaspoonful of mustard or Tabasco sauce to the bowl at step 3 to give the pâté a bit of a kick.

$^1/_2$ lb (225 g) chicken livers
1 onion

2 cloves of garlic
2 tsp thyme
2 tbsp butter
$^1/_2$ small glass of sherry or brandy
2 tbsp single cream

Method
1. Clean and cut the livers into small pieces, removing any skin or fatty bits then peel and finely chop the onion and crush the garlic.
2. Melt 1 tbsp butter in a large saucepan, add the liver, onion, garlic and thyme, and fry for about 5 minutes then turn the heat down, cover with a lid and cook gently for another 5 minutes.
3. Transfer everything to a large mixing bowl with a slotted spoon in order to leave most of the liquid behind in the pan.
4. Blend on the lowest speed setting for a minute, adding a fresh bit of butter (about 1 tbsp) with the sherry and cream and then blend for a few seconds more.
5. Put the pâté into a small casserole dish, or six small ramekins, and chill in the fridge for about an hour. Eat within four days.

BEEF STROGANOFF

Beef Stroganoff is traditionally made with fillet steak but you can use cheaper cuts of meat; all you need to do is cook the meat for longer.

$1^1/_2$–2 lb (roughly 1 kg) steak
1 medium onion

$^{1}/_{2}$ lb (225 g) button mushrooms
1 tsp mustard (preferably Dijon but French would do)
1 small (5 fl oz/150 ml) carton of single cream
2 tbsp sherry or brandy
Parsley
Butter
Oil
Salt & pepper

Method
1. Heat some oil in a large frying pan; cut the steak into fine strips (straight from the packet, don't wash it), sprinkle with a little salt and pepper and quick-fry for a minute to seal the meat on all sides before turning the heat right down and simmering very gently for about half an hour.
2. Add a good lump of butter to the pan and fry the finely chopped onions until soft and golden, then add the sliced mushrooms and cook for another 2 or 3 minutes.
3. Stir in the mustard with the brandy (or sherry) and cream, and warm through very gently to stop the cream curdling for 5–10 minutes.
4. Sprinkle with plenty of parsley and serve with plain boiled rice and salad.

ORANGES IN CARAMEL

As a rough guide, allow one orange per person plus one extra, and if you've got one of those little zester things that takes the rind off oranges and lemons in super-thin strips, use that; otherwise cut the rind into very fine strips with a sharp knife.

8 oranges
$^1/_2$ pint (300 ml) water
$^1/_2$ lb (225 g) sugar (white or soft brown)
Rind of one orange pared into thin strips
$^1/_2$ glass of sherry
1 tsp cinnamon

Method

1. Wash one orange in warm water and pare the rind into strips.
2. Peel the remaining oranges and make sure all the white pith is removed.
3. Slice the oranges into rounds, carefully picking out any pips (if there are any) and put the orange slices in a cut-glass bowl.
4. Put the water and sugar in a fairly large saucepan and heat gently and slowly for a few minutes until all the sugar has dissolved.
5. Once you're sure the sugar has dissolved completely, turn the heat up and let the liquid boil quite rapidly until you've got a golden brown syrup. (Don't overdo it though; the syrup can go from a perfect dark brown to burnt black in a few seconds.)
6. Remove the syrup from the heat and allow to cool for about 20 minutes.
7. Sprinkle the oranges with sherry and cinnamon then pour the syrup over the fruit and top with the strips of orange rind.
8. Cover the bowl with a plate and leave to stand at room temperature, or refrigerate.

TUNA PÂTÉ

MEDALLIONS OF LAMB IN RED WINE SAUCE

ORANGE JELLY CHEESECAKE

TUNA PÂTÉ

1 large tin of tuna
4 oz (100 g) butter
4 tbsp soft cream cheese or Quark
Lemon juice
Salt & pepper

Method
1. Put the butter in a bowl and beat until creamy (use a small hand whisk if you find it easier).
2. Add the rest of the ingredients and beat again to make a (fairly) smooth pâté.
3. Chill the pâté in the fridge for at least an hour; serve with small triangles of toast, crusts removed, and garnish with cucumber slices and tomato wedges.

MEDALLIONS OF LAMB IN RED WINE SAUCE

2 lb+ (1.5 kg) lamb neck fillet
1 red onion
Mushrooms
$^{1}/_{2}$ bottle red wine (or 1 whole small bottle)
Olive oil
Butter
Cornflour
Tomato purée
Garlic purée

Method

1. Cut the lamb neck fillet into thick medallions about $1^{1}/_{2}$ in (3 cm) thick.
2. Warm oil in a large, deep-sided pan, turn the heat up and quickly fry the lamb, browning on all sides.
3. Turn the heat down, strain the liquid out of the pan, replace with a couple of spoonfuls of fresh oil and some butter then add the finely chopped mushrooms and onion and cook gently for a few more minutes.
4. When the onions and butter are soft, pour the wine into the pan, stir well, cover the pan with a lid and simmer very gently for at least 1–$1^{1}/_{2}$ hours.
5. As soon as the lamb is tender turn the heat up and let the wine stock in the pan boil rapidly for a few minutes to reduce the liquid.
6. Dissolve a couple of teaspoons of cornflour in a small bowl with a teaspoon of cold water then mix in a dessertspoonful each of tomato and garlic purée and add about two dessertspoonfuls of hot liquid from the pan.

7. Turn the heat right down again, add the cornflour mixture to the pan, stir well and simmer for a couple of minutes.
8. Serve with any kind of potatoes and green vegetables.

ORANGE JELLY CHEESECAKE

Serves 4–6
1 orange jelly
$^1/_2$ lb (300 g) tub of soft cream cheese
2 tbsp Greek yoghurt, natural yoghurt or crème fraîche
8 large digestive biscuits
2 oz (50 g) butter
1 small tin mandarin segments

Method
1. Melt the butter in a saucepan, add the crushed digestive biscuits and blend together. Press the mixture into a lightly greased, loose-bottomed, round cake tin about 8 in (20 cm) across.
2. Put the jelly in a measuring jug with $^1/_2$ pint (approximately 250 ml) of boiling water and stir for a few minutes until dissolved. *Don't top up with cold water in the usual way*; add 2 or 3 ice cubes to cool the jelly down quickly, then leave it to stand for about 20 minutes. (If you don't have any ice just leave the jelly to stand in a cool place for a few minutes longer.)
3. Put the cream cheese in a large mixing bowl with the cool jelly and yoghurt (or crème fraîche) and beat it all together with an electric hand whisk for half a minute until smooth.
4. Spread the filling evenly over the biscuit base and leave to set in the fridge for at least 1 hour.
5. Decorate the top of the cheesecake with the mandarin segments and serve with cream if you have it.

COOL CUCUMBER SOUP

—◆—

SAUSAGES & WARM POTATO SALAD

—◆—

STRAWBERRIES & CREAM SPONGE

This would be a really easy option for a dinner party in the summer when strawberries are in season and the idea of cold soup isn't such a turn-off; the starter and dessert can both be made well in advance and there's very little preparation to do for the main course.

COOL CUCUMBER SOUP
—◆—

Needless to say, the flavour of the soup is greatly improved if you make it with real home-made chicken stock, as opposed to using a stock cube. On the other hand, you get a much prettier shade of green if you add a very few drops of green food colouring to the soup at the end.

2 large cucumbers
1 small onion
1 pint (600 ml) warm milk
$^1/_2$ pint (300 ml) chicken stock (1 stock cube)
1 tbsp plain flour
$^1/_2$ tsp nutmeg
Salt & pepper
Butter
1 small carton of single cream
Mint or parsley

Method

1. Peel and halve the cucumbers, scoop out the seedy bit in the middle and chop the cucumbers into chunks; also peel and roughly chop the onion.
2. Melt some butter in a large saucepan then fry the cucumber and onion for a few minutes before adding the flour and cooking for another minute, stirring all the time.
3. Take the pan off the heat while you warm the milk in another saucepan – or in a bowl in the microwave – and make $^1/_2$ pint (300 ml) of stock with 1 stock cube in a measuring jug, adding the nutmeg and seasoning to the hot stock. (If you're using fresh stock there's no need to warm it first, just make sure it's thawed properly if you've taken it from the freezer.)
4. Gradually pour the stock into the pan with the cucumbers and onion, followed by the warm milk, then put the pan over a moderate heat and bring to the boil, stirring continuously.
5. Turn the heat right down and simmer gently for about 20 minutes.
6. Allow the soup to cool for a few minutes then purée in a blender or food processor, adjusting the seasoning and adding a few drops of green food colouring if liked.
7. Chill the soup in the fridge for at least two hours; serve with a swirl of single cream if you have it and sprinkle with mint or parsley.

SAUSAGES & WARM POTATO SALAD

This main course would work just as well with gammon steaks or a joint of bacon, roasted or boiled and cut into thick slices, instead of sausages.

Good, thick sausages (min. 70% meat – say 2 per person)
4 medium-sized potatoes
4 eggs, hard-boiled
1 red onion
1 clove of garlic
1 red pepper (or any other colour will do if you don't have red)
Chives
Parsley
2 tbsp vinegar (preferably cider or white wine vinegar)
2 tbsp lemon juice
1 tsp Dijon mustard
Salt & black pepper

Method

1. Prick the sausages and cook them in the oven in a large greased dish on Gas Mark 6 (200°C) for about half an hour, or until they're a dark golden brown.
2. Meanwhile, boil potatoes in the usual way, preferably in their skins, and hard-boil the eggs (start in cold water, bring to the boil and simmer gently for 10 minutes).
3. With the sausages in the oven and the potatoes and eggs cooking, wash, de-seed and chop the pepper, finely chop the red onion, crush the garlic and make a dressing with the vinegar, lemon juice and mustard by mixing them all together in a cup.
4. Cut the potatoes and eggs into large chunks while everything is still very warm.
5. Put potatoes and eggs in a salad bowl then add the dressing, chopped pepper, finely chopped onion and crushed garlic and gently mix together.
6. Sprinkle with chives, parsley, salt and black pepper; serve with the sausages and warm sweetcorn or cold tomatoes cut into wedges.

STRAWBERRIES & CREAM SPONGE

Most basic creamed cake mixtures can be made using this easy all-in-one method, although it sometimes pays to follow the usual steps – i.e. beating the butter and sugar together till pale and fluffy then adding the eggs very gradually – especially if you're working with a larger quantity of ingredients and you want a guaranteed perfect result. But with fresh strawberries and cream you can get away with the soft option here, no question.

4 oz (100 g) butter or margarine
4 oz (100 g) caster sugar
4 oz (100 g) self-raising flour
1 teaspoon of baking powder
2 eggs
Fresh strawberries
Double cream
Icing sugar

Method
1. Grease and base line two sandwich tins (approx 7 in/18 cm) and preheat the oven to Gas Mark 3–4 (170–180ºC).
2. Put the flour, baking powder, butter, sugar and eggs in a large bowl and beat thoroughly together for about 1 minute, preferably using an electric hand whisk.
3. Divide the mixture evenly between the two prepared cake tins and bake in the centre of the oven (or centre and lower middle if you can't fit both tins on the same shelf) for about 30 minutes, until the cakes are golden on top and springy to the touch.
4. Allow to cool completely while you wash, dry and cut the strawberries into halves or quarters. Add a couple of teaspoons

of sugar to the double cream and whip till just thick and firm enough; if the cream looks holey you've gone too far.

5. Sandwich the sponges together with a mixture of the chopped strawberries and cream and top the cake with more of the same. Dust with icing sugar to finish.

Tip

Save the paper wrappers from blocks of butter, margarine and lard and use to grease oven trays and cake tins.

EGG & BACON SALAD

BAKED FISH IN HORSERADISH SAUCE

GOOSEBERRY FOOL

This is a nice easy one to do if you've been at work all day and haven't had time to prepare anything in advance as it probably only takes a little over an hour from start to finish. Make the gooseberry fool first, followed by the bacon and egg salad, and keep them both in the fridge. The salad can be served as the fish goes into the oven; by the time you've eaten it the main course will be ready.

EGG & BACON SALAD

1 packet of streaky bacon ($^1/_2$ lb/250 g)
4 eggs, hard-boiled
1 bunch of spring onions

1 iceberg lettuce
2 radishes
4 tbsp vinegar
4 tsp sugar
Parsley
Sesame seeds
Oil
Salt & pepper

Method
1. Hard-boil the eggs in the usual way while you snip the bacon into smallish pieces and fry in a large pan till crisp and golden.
2. Remove the bacon from the pan with a slotted spoon and leave to cool quickly on a large plate. (Cool the cooked hard-boiled eggs in cold water.)
3. Fry the chopped spring onions and a handful of sesame seeds in the same oil, adding a little more oil or a tablespoon of butter if you think the pan's too dry, then cook for a couple of minutes till the onions are slightly soft.
4. Stir in the vinegar and sugar with a couple of tablespoons of water and bring to the boil.
5. Take the pan off the heat as soon as the liquid boils; pour the contents into another container and leave to cool.
6. Meanwhile, wash and shred the lettuce and mix with the finely sliced radishes in a salad bowl.
7. Add the bacon to the salad bowl and pour over the cooled onion dressing. Top with the chopped hard-boiled eggs, sprinkle with parsley and season with salt and pepper.

BAKED FISH IN HORSERADISH SAUCE WITH PARMESAN & PAPRIKA POTATOES

I normally make this with thick, white fresh fish (pollack is ideal) but because the lovely flavour of the sauce acts as a camouflage for the cheapest frozen fillets, I sometimes use those as well. (And, needless to say, at the other end of the scale this recipe works equally well with fresh tuna or salmon steaks.)

If you don't have horseradish – or you hate it – use wholegrain mustard instead.

1 or 2 good-size pieces of fish per person
2–3 tbsp horseradish cream
1–2 tbsp natural yoghurt
2 tsp cornflour
Lemon juice
Potatoes
Fresh Parmesan cheese
Paprika
Oil

Method

1. Wash the fish and arrange in a large ovenproof dish or casserole (it doesn't matter if the pieces of fish overlap slightly) while you preheat the oven to Gas Mark 6 (200°C).
2. Blend the horseradish, yoghurt and cornflour with plenty of lemon juice, coat the fish then cover and leave to stand while you peel the potatoes and dice them into small chunks.
3. Put the potatoes in a large pan of cold water and bring to the boil in the usual way while you warm some oil in another large ovenproof dish. Once the water's boiling, only allow the

potatoes to simmer for about one minute; the chunks are small and you don't want them turning to mush.

4. Drain the potatoes and rinse thoroughly in cold water in the pan, then drain them again and toss them in as much grated Parmesan and paprika as you like.

5. Bake the potatoes in the hot oil for about 15 minutes at the top of the oven then put the fish near the bottom of the oven for about 20 minutes, by which time the potatoes should be perfectly crisp and golden.

6. Serve with salad, green vegetables or sweetcorn and garnish with tomatoes sprinkled with chives and vinaigrette.

GOOSEBERRY FOOL

This is so easy it's embarrassing, but who cares? When you've already made two other courses (almost) from scratch, you don't need an excuse for anything. (Use another type of tinned fruit – rhubarb, for instance – if you don't like gooseberries, and sweeten the fool with an extra tablespoon of caster sugar if you like.)

2 tins of gooseberries in natural juice or syrup
1 large carton of ready-made custard
1 large carton of double cream
2 tsp vanilla extract
1 heaped tbsp caster sugar

Method

1. Purée the fruit in a blender or food processor with about half the juice or syrup from the tin, then put the fruit in a large bowl with the custard and mix well.

2. Whip the double cream in another bowl until it's firm enough

to hold its shape and stand up in stiff peaks, then combine thoroughly with the gooseberries and custard, adding the vanilla extract and sugar according to taste.

3. Divide into individual glasses or bowls and chill in the fridge for at least two hours.

AUBERGINE DIP

ORANGE BAKED CHICKEN

SWEET PASTRIES

AUBERGINE DIP

Tahini paste is easy enough to find in most supermarkets, but if you can't get it for any reason, whiz a small packet of sesame seeds in a food processor with a few tablespoons of olive oil instead. (You can also make pretty good – if not authentic – hummus without tahini paste in a similar way.)

2–3 aubergines
2 cloves of garlic
1 small jar of tahini paste
Lemon juice
Salt & black pepper
Black olives
Mini pitta breads or unflavoured tortilla chips

Method

1. Bake the aubergines in a moderate oven – say, Gas Mark 5 (190°C) – for 20–30 minutes until they feel like they're soft inside.
2. Once they're cool enough to handle, peel the skins off the aubergines and pulse them in a blender or food processor with the crushed garlic, tahini paste and lemon juice to taste.
3. Adjust the seasoning with salt and black pepper, transfer the dip to a shallow serving bowl and chill in the fridge for at least a couple of hours.
4. Serve with black olives and pitta bread or plain tortilla chips.

ORANGE BAKED CHICKEN

Cook the chicken with or without the skin, whichever way you like it.

6–8 chicken pieces
$^1/_2$ mug of orange juice
1 onion
2 tbsp soy sauce or Worcestershire sauce
2 tbsp tomato purée
1 tsp coriander
1 tsp coriander leaf
1 tsp sugar
Oil
Butter

Method

1. Take a sheet of kitchen foil big enough to cover the bottom of a large ovenproof dish with enough foil around the sides to fold over and make a parcel once the chicken is inside.

2. Warm a little oil in a large frying pan; brown the chicken pieces on all sides, then transfer to the foil-lined dish.

3. Add some butter to the pan and let it melt and brown to the point where it's nearly foaming then put the finely chopped onion in the pan with the coriander and coriander leaf and fry for a minute or two until soft but without colour.

4. Add the orange juice, tomato purée, soy (or Worcestershire) sauce and sugar, stir well and bring to the boil.

5. Pour the sauce over the chicken, cover with the foil and cook on Gas Mark 3 (170°C) for about 1 hour, spooning the sauce over the chicken on the plate at the end.

6. Serve with fried potatoes and green vegetables.

SWEET PASTRIES

These little pastries are so simple to make but look and taste almost like something from a proper baker or patisserie.

Instead of sugar and spice try chocolate spread or apricot jam as fillings – or make a mixture of all three.

Finally, although I always make dough by hand in a mixing bowl rather than bother with a food processor, this recipe is significantly quicker and easier if you make the dough by whizzing the ingredients together electronically, so this is one time it's worth the extra washing up.

5 oz (125 g) plain flour
4 oz (100 g) butter or margarine
4 oz (100 g) soft cream cheese
2 tbsp sour cream (or 2 tbsp regular cream + 1 tsp lemon juice)
4 tbsp icing sugar
1 tsp mixed spice
1 tsp cinnamon
1 big tbsp of butter (for the filling)

Method

1. Put the flour, butter or margarine, soft cream cheese and sour cream together in a food processor or electric mixer then whiz or pulse for a couple of minutes until the mixture forms a soft dough.
2. Divide the dough into two halves, wrap each half in cling film, foil or a large food bag and chill in the fridge for about an hour.
3. Melt the butter for the filling in a small bowl or mug and sift the icing sugar and spices together in another bowl.
4. Preheat the oven to Gas Mark 4 (180ºC) and lightly grease 2 baking sheets before you roll out each piece of dough into a rough circle large enough to cut round a dinner plate. (Save the trimmings for re-rolling.)
5. Cut each circle of dough into approximately 10–12 wedges, like a pizza, and brush each wedge with melted butter.
6. Sprinkle the mixed icing sugar and spices over the wedges and roll each one into a twist, starting with the widest part and gently pressing the pointed tip into the dough at the end.
7. Bake in the oven for 20–25 minutes until golden and leave the pastries to cool on the trays for a few minutes before transferring to a wire rack to cool completely.

STUFFED MUSHROOMS

CLASSIC SPAGHETTI BOLOGNESE

AMARETTI PEACHES

STUFFED MUSHROOMS

Normally I don't bother to dry out breadcrumbs, I just whiz the bread in the food processor and freeze the breadcrumbs as they are, but this recipe works better if the breadcrumbs are nice and crisp. The easiest way to do this is to spread the breadcrumbs out on a large tray and put them in the oven on Gas Mark 6 (200°C) for 3 or 4 minutes. (Bash them up in the bag first if they've been frozen, leave to stand at room temperature for about 20 minutes then crumble them up completely with your hands.)

1 or 2 large flat-cap mushrooms per person
Crispy white breadcrumbs
Fresh Parmesan cheese
Garlic purée
Vegetable stock
Olive oil
Parsley

Method
1. Wash and peel the mushrooms and remove the stalks completely.
2. Make up about $^1/_2$ pint (300 ml) of stock with $^1/_2$ a stock cube

or a teaspoonful of Marmite or Vegemite and poach the mushrooms in the stock for five minutes.

3. Put the warm mushrooms on an oven tray, spread each one with a generous squeeze of garlic purée topped with a mixture of breadcrumbs and finely grated Parmesan; drizzle with olive oil and grill for a few minutes until the toppings are crisp and brown.

4. Sprinkle with parsley and serve.

CLASSIC SPAGHETTI BOLOGNESE

The number one favourite in the late seventies and early eighties, Spaghetti Bolognese is so far out of fashion as dinner party food these days it's about to stage a comeback (remember, you read it here first).

Anyway, there are two types of Spaghetti Bolognese; the kind you make in five minutes flat with a packet of mince and a jar of instant sauce, and the real deal which includes bacon, chicken livers and, of course, wine – traditionally white, although red does the job just as well.

1lb + (500 g) minced beef
6 rashers of back bacon
Small packet or tub of chicken livers
1 onion
2 cloves of garlic
1 carrot
2 tins of chopped tomatoes
Tomato purée
1 beef stock cube
$^1/_4$ pint (150 ml) of dry white wine (approx)
Oregano or Italian herbs

Method

1. Cut the chicken livers into halves or quarters, snip the bacon into small pieces and trim the fat.

2. Put all the meat into a very large pan over a high heat, breaking up the mince with a wooden spoon.

3. When the meat is just cooked through, almost cover the pan with a lid then tip the pan and carefully strain off as much of the fatty liquid as you can.

4. Add the crushed garlic, a finely chopped onion, grated carrot and herbs and cook for a few more minutes.

5. Crumble a stock cube into the pan, add the chopped tomatoes with about half a tube of tomato purée, pour in the wine, give it all a good stir then cover with a lid and cook on a low heat for about half an hour. (Thicken the Bolognese with more tomato purée, or if you want to thin it down, use more wine or a mixture of beef stock and wine.)

6. Serve with spaghetti. Obviously. And if, like me, you don't enjoy messing about with long strands of spaghetti – and you hate watching other people messing about with long strands of spaghetti – break it into much smaller pieces before cooking so you can just fork it up without trailing it all over your chin first. (I mean, what's the point?)

AMARETTI PEACHES IN WHITE WINE

Use nectarines if you don't like the texture of peach skin. Otherwise, you could just remove the skin (or use tinned peaches) but you lose some of the colour this way, which spoils the overall look of the fruit. Allow roughly one biscuit for each peach half, but quantities don't have to be exact, this is another one of those failsafe recipes that seems to work every which way. (Any type of almond biscuits or macaroons will do if you can't get Amaretti.)

6–8 peaches or nectarines
8–10 Amaretti biscuits
2 oz (50 g) butter (preferably unsalted)
2 oz (50 g) caster or icing sugar
$^1\!/_2$ pint (300 ml) white wine

Method
1. Wash the peaches and cut them in half then carefully remove the stones.
2. Use a knife or teaspoon to scoop a little of the flesh out of each half, making the hollows deep enough to take the filling, then put the bits of removed fruit in a bowl and chop them up a bit more.
3. Soften the butter in the microwave then add to the bowl with half the sugar and the crushed Amaretti biscuits, mixing everything together well.
4. Place the peach halves in a lightly buttered, deep-sided ovenproof dish and stuff them with filling.
5. Pour the wine over and around the peaches and sprinkle the remainder of the sugar over the fruit. Bake in a preheated oven on Gas Mark 4 (180°C) for about half an hour until the fruit is tender.
6. Serve warm or cold, with or without single cream.

POTATO SKINS

PORK IN PICKLE SAUCE

PROFITEROLES IN COFFEE SAUCE

Not one for a busy week night unless you get home before 5 p.m. and have already prepped the potato skins and profiteroles in advance.

This is a very good menu price-wise, though. You only need to buy one large carton of double cream; about two thirds of that can be whipped and used to fill the profiteroles and the rest can be made into sour cream with approximately 1 tablespoon of lemon juice. The pork fillets, potatoes, vegetables and eggs are all still very affordable, and basic store cupboard ingredients account for the rest of the menu.

POTATO SKINS WITH SOUR CREAM & HOT TOMATO DIP

Once the skins have been removed, mash the remainder of the potatoes to go with the pork, adding a little sour cream and a couple of egg yolks or some grated cheese, and seasoning with salt and pepper.

An even quicker way of making potato skins is to wash and carve slices off the uncooked potatoes and *then* bake or deep-fry them. It still works, but the texture isn't as good as it is when you boil the potatoes in their skins first. (Buy a jar of hot salsa dip if you don't have time to make your own.)

2 medium-sized potatoes per person (approximately)
Salt
Sour cream

For the Hot Tomato Dip
1 tin of chopped tomatoes
$^1/_2$ small jar of mayonnaise
1 large onion
2 cloves of garlic
$^1/_2$ tsp chilli powder
Salt & pepper
(Tabasco or Worcestershire sauce)
Oil

Method
1. Give the potatoes a quick wash in cold water with a nail-brush then put them in a saucepan with fresh cold water, bring to the boil in the usual way and simmer gently for about 15 minutes until the potatoes are cooked through. (A sharp knife should go easily through the potato when it's done.)
2. When the potatoes are cool enough to handle, carve the peel off in thick slices from top to bottom and lightly season the potato skins with salt.
3. Sprinkle the skins with oil and bake in a preheated oven, Gas Mark 7 (220°C) for about 20 minutes until golden.
4. Serve warm with the hot tomato dip and sour cream.

To make the Hot Tomato Dip
1. Warm some oil in a pan then fry the finely chopped onion and crushed garlic for a few minutes until just soft.
2. Add the chilli powder and chopped tomatoes, turn the heat up and bring to the boil, stirring continuously.
3. Simmer for about 20 minutes until the liquid reduces slightly and the sauce thickens, then remove from the heat and allow to cool for about half an hour before adjusting the seasoning with salt and pepper and a little Tabasco or Worcestershire sauce if liked.

4. Mix the tomato sauce in a bowl with the mayonnaise, cover with cling film and keep in the fridge.

PORK IN PICKLE SAUCE

While the pork is cooking – and before you make the sauce – put ice-cream-scoop-sized dollops of mashed potato on a flat baking tray lined with greased greaseproof paper and score lightly with a fork all the way round to tart them up a bit. Or pipe the potato through a star-shaped nozzle if you have enough time and patience – not to mention a piping bag. In fact, you can make a fairly good piping bag yourself by twisting a large semicircle of greaseproof paper into a cone shape then securing with Sellotape all the way along the join and snipping off the pointed end, but only work with small amounts of potato if you're using a home-made piping bag; mashed potatoes are a lot heavier than cream or meringue and too much will burst the bag. (You'll still need the star-shaped nozzle for this to work though.)

2 thin pork fillets per person
1 cucumber
$^{1}/_{2}$ onion
$^{1}/_{2}$ pint (250 ml) pale stock (chicken or vegetable)
Milk
Butter
2 tbsp flour
$^{1}/_{2}$ tsp nutmeg
$^{1}/_{2}$ very small jar of pickled gherkins (with vinegar)

Method

1. Grill or fry the pork fillets for a few minutes to brown the outside then transfer the meat to a casserole dish, cover tightly with foil and bake in a preheated oven, Gas Mark 3 (170°C), while you make the sauce.

2. Now peel and de-seed the cucumber and chop it into chunks; also peel and chop the onion while you warm some butter in a frying pan. When it's just about foaming, add the cucumber and onion and cook gently for a few minutes until the onion has softened but not coloured.

3. Add the flour and nutmeg to the pan, stirring well, and cook for another minute. (Take the pan off the heat while you make the stock.)

4. Make the stock in a measuring jug (with one stock cube) to *barely* 1/2 pint (about 250 ml), adding a splash of milk and 1–2 tbsp of vinegar from the jar of gherkins.

5. Add the stock to the pan, stirring well. Bring to the boil then simmer gently for a couple of minutes, stirring constantly until the sauce thickens.

6. Allow the sauce to cool slightly then blend in a food processor or liquidizer.

7. Cut roughly half the jar of gherkins into slices and add them to the sauce.

8. Pour the sauce over the pork fillets then cover with the foil again and cook for another 30 minutes or so until the pork is completely tender.

9. Serve with creamed potatoes (see above) and green vegetables or salad.

PROFITEROLES IN COFFEE SAUCE

If you make profiteroles regularly you know exactly how the dough should look at every stage; otherwise you can't always tell if you've beaten the mixture too hard or added too much egg until it's too late.

But apart from that it's all good news. Profiteroles are fantastic value for money, take only minutes to make and are loved by almost everyone. The only slightly fiddly thing is you *will* need a piping bag to get the cream inside at the end, but the uncooked profiteroles don't have to be piped, they can be spooned onto the baking sheets by hand.

Don't worry if your profiteroles aren't identical to the ones you find in the supermarket either. We're so used to synthetic, mass-produced desserts it's easy not to realize that the home-made version only looks slightly different because actually it's even better. As long as the profiteroles are cooked properly inside it doesn't matter if they're not exactly a work of art, and piled into glass bowls and covered in sauce it's hard to tell anyway.

I always use one very large egg instead of two medium ones. You have to add the egg gradually so the dough doesn't become too slack (see below) but I've found that if you just use one very large egg instead of two smaller ones, you won't even have to worry about overdoing it.

Finally, although you can use plain flour to make profiteroles, it's a good idea to use strong bread flour, which is much more robust and really helps the profiteroles to hold their shape.

You'll get about 18 profiteroles from this mixture, which would serve about four people.

2 oz (50 g) butter or margarine
$^1/_4$ pint (150 ml) water
3 oz (75 g) strong bread flour
2 eggs, beaten (or 1 very large, see above)
$^2/_3$ large carton of double cream, whipped

For the sauce
1 oz (25 g) butter or margarine
1 big tbsp golden syrup
1 tsp instant coffee dissolved in 2 tbsp boiling water
1 egg, beaten
6 oz (150 g) icing sugar

Method

1. Preheat the oven to Gas Mark 5 (190ºC) and lightly grease a couple of large baking sheets with a few drops of oil and water.
2. Put the butter or margarine in a saucepan with $^1/_4$ pint (150 ml) of water; heat fairly gently until the fat has melted then bring to the boil.
3. Immediately the water is boiling take the pan off the heat, tip the flour in all at once and start beating with a wooden spoon. As soon as the dough starts coming together put the pan back over the heat and continue beating until the dough forms a rough ball in the middle of the pan. This will only take about a minute, so don't overdo it or the dough will become too fatty.
4. Now put the dough straight into a mixing bowl and allow it to cool for a couple of minutes. At this stage you can either continue beating the dough with a wooden spoon, which is very hard work, or use an electric hand whisk. (Or even put the dough into a food processor and add the eggs through the funnel.)

5. Add the beaten egg *a little at a time* as you beat the dough vigorously. At this stage you want to incorporate as much air as you can, which is what gives the profiteroles their light texture. When the dough is still firm with a sheen on the surface it's ready. If you add too much egg the dough becomes too slack and the profiteroles won't have such a good shape or consistency.

6. Spoon the dough onto the baking sheets to make 18 profiteroles roughly the size of a peach stone and bake in the oven for 25–30 minutes until well risen and golden.

7. Allow to cool completely, then fill the profiteroles with whipped cream by making a small hole in the bottom or side of each one with a very sharp knife, a skewer or the end of a corkscrew.

To make the sauce

(To make a chocolate sauce, replace the coffee with a 4 oz (100 g) bar of plain chocolate).

Method

1. In a medium-sized bowl dissolve 1 heaped teaspoon of instant coffee in a couple of tablespoons of boiling water, add the butter or margarine and the golden syrup and melt the whole lot over a saucepan of hot water.

2. Take the bowl off the heat, add the egg and sift in the icing sugar, then beat at high speed with an electric hand whisk for about 30 seconds until you've got a thick, smooth icing.

3. Arrange the profiteroles in one large bowl or several small ones and put them in the fridge while you wait for the sauce to cool for half an hour. (The sauce can also be put in the fridge.)

4. Spoon some of the sauce over the profiteroles and keep the rest in a jug to serve hot or cold with the profiteroles at the end.

PRAWN COCKTAIL

BLADE BEEF STEAK & CHIPS

BLACK FOREST GATEAU

Back to the seventies again (see Classic Spaghetti Bolognese).

The steak should ideally be sirloin, or even fillet, but when you can't afford to fork out for Desperate Dan-sized T-bones for each person there's always blade beef, which, cooked slowly and carefully, will still give you a good result, especially when it's served with a nice sauce. Blade beef from the shoulder of the cow is very good value for money, and if it isn't already carved up on the tray, your friendly local butcher will gladly cut it into thick steaks for you to take home. (Unfortunately, you probably won't find blade beef in the supermarket.)

And could any other meal be quite so retro or more of a cliché than this one? Any minute now we'll be having a fondue party …

PRAWN COCKTAIL

There's more than one way to make a prawn cocktail; this is the most basic version, which I think is all you need with two other courses on the menu.

The quantities given below are enough for up to six prawn cocktails and any surplus cucumber, lettuce and tomato can be used to make a garnish or small side salad to go with the main course.

Small bag of frozen prawns (defrosted)
$^1/_2$ small iceberg lettuce
$^1/_2$ cucumber

1 smallish tomato per person
1 lemon
Lemon juice
4 generous tbsp tomato ketchup
Ditto mayonnaise or salad cream
Paprika

Method
1. In six wine glasses (or similar), wash and finely shred the iceberg, and make a little bed of lettuce at the bottom of each glass.
2. Wash and slice the cucumber and tomatoes any way you like and mix with the lettuce, leaving about $\frac{1}{2}$ in (1.25 cm) of room in each glass for the prawns.
3. Blend the ketchup and mayonnaise together with a little lemon juice; fill the glasses to the brim with prawns, top with the dressing and sprinkle with a little paprika.
4. Cut the whole lemon in half and take out the pithy centre by cutting a small V shape either side of the core. Cut each half of lemon into two or three wedges, carefully remove the pips and put a piece of lemon on each glass. Serve with thin slices of brown bread and butter cut into small triangles, crusts removed.

BLADE BEEF STEAK & CHIPS

Blade beef steaks
$\frac{1}{2}$ pint (300 ml) of beef stock
$\frac{1}{2}$ glass of sherry
1 tsp mustard
Salt and black pepper

Onions or shallots
Mushrooms
1^1/$_2$ tbsp flour
Butter
Oil

Method

1. Put the steaks between a large folded sheet of greaseproof paper and bash hard with a meat hammer or large rolling pin for a few minutes to tenderize the steaks and flatten them out as much as you can. Season with salt and black pepper.
2. Warm a couple of teaspoons of oil in a large frying pan and as soon as the pan is really hot, wipe dry with kitchen roll (don't burn your fingers) and put the steaks in the pan two at a time, pressing the meat down hard with a slice in order to seal and brown the steaks as quickly as you can. (This won't take any longer than 20–30 seconds on each side.)
3. Transfer the steaks to a very large casserole or ovenproof dish and pour on the stock mixed with the sherry and mustard; cover with a lid or a layer of foil and cook in a low preheated oven, say Gas Mark 2 (160ºC), for about 1^1/$_2$ hours.
4. Towards the end of the cooking time fry the onions and mushrooms in butter over a low heat, and once the steaks are tender, keep them warm and covered at the bottom of the oven while you pour the stock into a clean saucepan or measuring jug.
5. Sift the flour into the pan with the onions and mushrooms and stir well for a minute before pouring the stock into the pan, stirring all the time.
6. Pour the sauce over the steaks on the plate and serve with chips, peas and salad.

BLACK FOREST GATEAU

This recipe should ideally contain six eggs but I've made it with only four eggs before and it's still good. The raw mixture has a bit less volume, that's all, meaning you get a slightly smaller cake. I normally use Cadbury's Flakes but it has to be said, Black Forest Gateau lacks class without proper grated dark chocolate curls ... so you decide. (Flakes come in packs of five at the supermarket, which is about right.)

And if you haven't got kirsch you'll know exactly what to use instead – assuming you've already read some of the other recipes in this book ... (That would be sherry. What else?)

Finally, classic Black Forest Gateau consists of three layers, so you should really make one large cake and cut it into three when the sponges are cool, but I much prefer making layered cakes in separate sandwich tins because not only do they cook more quickly, evenly and reliably that way, it saves you the hassle of trying to cut them up neatly afterwards. The really lazy way to do it – i.e. my way – is to just make the cake in two sandwich tins and settle for two layers.

4 oz (100 g) butter or margarine
6 oz (150 g) plain flour
2 tsp baking powder
2 oz (50 g) cocoa powder
6 oz (150 g) caster sugar
6 eggs (or 4 – see above)
2 tins of black cherries in heavy syrup
4 tbsp kirsch *or* sherry
Cornflour
Small carton of whipping or double cream
$^1/_2$ lb (225 g) bar of dark chocolate
or Cadbury's Flakes

Method

1. Grease and base line however many cakes tins you're using and preheat the oven to Gas Mark 4 (180ºC).

2. Melt the butter until it's very, very soft – about 20 seconds in the microwave. (It doesn't have to be completely liquid, although that's okay.)

3. Put the eggs and sugar in a large bowl and beat with an electric hand whisk for a few minutes until the mixture is thick enough to leave a trail across the surface.

4. Sift in the flour, baking powder and cocoa powder; fold in gently (preferably with a large metal spoon) then add the melted butter and gently incorporate that into the mixture too.

5. Scoop the mixture equally into the prepared cake tins and bake in a moderate oven, Gas Mark 4 (180ºC) for about 20 minutes. (Check after 15 minutes if you're dividing the cake mixture into three tins, or if you've got a very hot oven; it varies.)

6. While the cakes are cooking, strain the cherry syrup into a small saucepan, add the kirsch (or sherry) and warm over a moderate heat until the liquid is near boiling point.

7. Put a couple of tablespoons of the liquid in a cup or small bowl with 2 teaspoons of cornflour, blend well then add the cornflour and syrup mixture to the syrup in the pan and stir over a reduced heat for a few more minutes until the syrup thickens slightly.

8. Allow to cool, then mix the cherries with the syrup. Meanwhile, whisk the cream in a separate bowl until it's thick enough. (Try not to overwhisk the cream to the point where it starts to look holey.)

9. Sandwich the sponges together with some of the cherries and cream, then spread more cream across the top and around the sides of the cake.

10. Put the remainder of the cherries on top of the cake, leaving about an inch (2 cm) around the edge; cover the top edge and sides of the cake all over with the crushed up Flakes or grated chocolate.

"A balanced diet is a cookie in each hand."

Barbara Johnson

5
Something sweet

Perhaps puddings aren't a strictly necessary part of a balanced diet – although plenty of them contain fruit and other nutritious ingredients such as eggs and milk – but the appeal of puddings and desserts is obvious really, and even when I can't think of a single reason for eating one, I can never think of a good enough reason not to …

GIPSY TART

An old school dinner favourite, Gipsy Tart was never the healthiest thing on the menu, but it's probably still less calorific than a turkey twizzler. At least there are vitamins in the evaporated milk, and putting a layer of thinly sliced bananas at the bottom ups the nutrient quotient even further.

You must make this the day before you want to eat it, though. It only takes a few minutes in the oven but you'll need to leave it in the fridge overnight for the filling to set into a kind of mousse.

Make it the ultimate easy-to-do pudding by buying ready-made pastry cases. The quantities here are enough for two Gipsy Tarts.

2 ready-made sweet pastry cases
1 tin of evaporated milk
$^1/_2$ mug of dark brown muscovado sugar
2–3 bananas

Method

1. Put the evaporated milk in a large bowl with the sugar and mix with an electric hand whisk on high speed for 5–10 minutes until the mixture is noticeably thicker.
2. Put a layer of thinly sliced banana at the bottom of the pastry case and fill each one to the top with the evaporated milk mixture.
3. Bake in a preheated oven on Gas Mark 6 (200ºC) for about 10 minutes until the surface of the tarts is firm to the touch and golden. (The inside will be pure liquid though, so don't be tempted to cut it open yet.)
4. Refrigerate overnight.

STEAMED SYRUP SPONGE

Steamed sponge puddings can just as easily be made with a couple of tablespoons of jam (any flavour, but raspberry or apricot would both be perfect) instead of the golden syrup.

This easy little recipe can be put together in minutes – you don't even have to weigh the ingredients – and while it's steaming away quietly at the back of the stove you can make dinner, eat dinner and paint your toenails by the time it's ready.

8 tbsp (8 oz/200 g) self-raising flour
4 tbsp (4 oz/100 g) butter or margarine
4 tbsp sugar
1 egg
$^1/_2$ cup of milk
2 tbsp golden syrup

Method

1. Grease an average-sized pudding basin or Pyrex bowl with butter or margarine ('average' would hold approximately $1\frac{1}{2}$–2 pints/850 ml–1 litre of water) and put a circle of greaseproof paper at the bottom of the basin.

2. Sift the flour into a large mixing bowl, add the butter or margarine in small pieces and rub in the fat until the mixture resembles medium-fine breadcrumbs.

3. Stir in the sugar.

4. Add the egg to $\frac{1}{2}$ cup of milk, whisk with a fork then pour into the bowl with the rest of the ingredients, mixing thoroughly to a smooth dropping consistency.

5. Put 2 big tablespoons of golden syrup at the bottom of the pudding basin then add the sponge mixture, smoothing the top with the back of the spoon and making a slight hollow at the centre.

6. Cover the pudding basin with a square of greaseproof paper and foil (greaseproof paper next to the pudding, foil on the outside) with a pleat in the middle and secure with a piece of string or Sellotape.

7. Steam the pudding in a large saucepan of boiling water for about $1\frac{1}{2}$ hours (the water should be about three quarters of the way up the basin) and check the level of the water every half hour or so to make sure the pan doesn't boil dry.

8. When cooked, remove the foil and greaseproof paper, hold a plate over the basin and tip it upside down so the pudding slides out onto the plate. Serve with single cream or custard.

LEMON MERINGUE PIE

People often think of lemon meringue pie as a fiddly dessert but it isn't at all, and if you use a ready-made flan case you can make it in a few minutes flat.

That said, the ready-made flan cases you find in the supermarket are about 8–9 in (20–23 cm) in diameter and very shallow, whereas the pastry case you'd make yourself in a flan tin that size (or slightly larger) would be deeper, so if you do use a ready-made flan case you'll have a bit too much meringue with these quantities, in which case you could either make a couple of meringue nests with the leftovers (just spoon the meringue onto a sheet of greaseproof paper on a separate oven tray and bake for the same length of time as the pie) or make the Simple Pineapple Sorbet (page 279) at the same time and use up the extra egg whites in that.

You can also use 2 whole lemons instead of 4 and make up the rest with bottled lemon juice instead, and although you should really cook the lemony bit in a double boiler, i.e. in a bowl over a pan of hot water, you can just as easily make it straight in the saucepan; just keep your eyes on it and don't let the sauce stick.

1 ready-made pastry case
or
6 oz (150 g) plain flour
3 oz (75 g) butter or margarine (or 1$^1/_2$ oz/40 g each of butter and lard)
1 heaped tbsp caster sugar
4–6 tbsp cold water (or a mixture of water and milk)

4 eggs, separated
6 heaped tbsp caster sugar

4 whole lemons (or 2 lemons + lemon juice)
2 tbsp cornflour
6 tbsp cold water

Method

1. To make your own pastry case, grease a flan dish or loose-bottomed cake tin and preheat the oven to Gas Mark 4 (180ºC); sift the flour into a mixing bowl, add the fat in small pieces and rub in until the mixture resembles medium-fine breadcrumbs then stir in the sugar, make a well in the centre and add the liquid, pinching the mixture together with your fingers to make a dough. Knead the dough for a minute then roll it out to fit the flan dish and bake 'blind' for about 15 minutes with a circle of greaseproof on the base, weighed down with rice or lentils to keep the pastry flat.

2. Separate the eggs. Put the yolks in a small saucepan with half the sugar and the grated rind and all the juice from the lemons and beat together with a wooden spoon.

3. Put the pan over a very low heat until all the sugar has melted; meanwhile, mix the cornflour and water together in a small cup or bowl to make a paste.

4. Add a couple of tablespoons of the liquid from the pan to the cornflour paste, blend well then pour the whole lot back into the pan; turn the heat up a bit and stir constantly for a couple of minutes until the lemon mixture turns into a fairly thick gel.

5. Scoop the lemon mixture into the pastry case.

6. Whisk the eggs whites with half the remainder of the sugar for a couple of minutes until the meringue is very stiff and standing up in peaks then add the rest of the sugar, folding it in with a large metal spoon.

7. Top the pie with the meringue, making sure the meringue meets the pastry around the edge of the pie without any gaps,

then bake the pie in a very low oven – Gas Mark 1 (120°C) for about an hour – check after 45 minutes – until the meringue is firmly set on top and just golden in places.

RICE PUDDING

Most people who think they hate rice pudding were put off by the stuff they had at school, but it's worth giving this one more try because apart from being cheap and good for children it's really quite nice; and perfect for those times you've already got the oven on a low heat for a few hours to cook a pot roast, or something else which takes as long.

You can make rice pudding with plain milk but I prefer it made with part fresh milk and a tin of evaporated milk, which gives it a bit more sweetness and a creamier texture. (Use any size tin you like and top up with the ordinary milk.)

4 oz (100 g) short-grain pudding rice
1 tin of evaporated milk
2–3 tablespoons sugar
Nutmeg
Milk
Butter

Method
1. Grease a shallow ovenproof dish with a little butter.
2. Pour the evaporated milk into a large measuring jug and make up to the 2 pint (1 litre) mark with plain milk.
3. Mix the rice and sugar with the milk mixture in the ovenproof dish, sprinkle with nutmeg and bake at the bottom of a low oven, Gas Mark 2 (150–160°C) for 2–3 hours or until the rice

is creamy and the top of the pudding is slightly golden.

4. Serve on its own, with jam, or with stewed fruit or bananas and a little more evaporated milk or single cream.

DIME BAR CAKE

Another ripped off Ikea favourite (see also Swedish Meatballs & Cream Sauce in 'Comfort Food'), the Dime Bar cake recipe – or Daim Bar as it's apparently called in Sweden – is such a closely guarded secret that all you have to do is look at the ingredients on the back of the box to be able to work out more or less how it's made, although I think the home-made version is better.

My very good friend Carole, an ace almond biscuit maker, came up with the idea of using soft cream cheese or Quark instead of buttercream, which is not only lower in fat, it makes the finished cake less sweet and sickly, but if you prefer to use buttercream, blend about 1 oz (25 g) of butter and 3 oz (75 g) of icing sugar with 1 tsp of vanilla essence and 1 tbsp of water.

Result.

4 large egg whites
4 oz (100 g) soft brown sugar
1 large packet of ground almonds: approximately 8 oz (200 g)
4 tsp vanilla essence
$^1/_2$ tsp salt
Half an 8 oz (225 g) tub of Quark or soft cream cheese
3 Dime bars

Method

1. Base line two average-sized loose-bottomed cake tins with greaseproof paper.
2. Whisk the egg whites with an electric hand whisk until the meringue is stiff enough to stand up in peaks and stays put when you turn the bowl upside down. (Takes about 2 minutes.)
3. Stir in the sugar, ground almonds and 2 tsp of vanilla essence and $^1/_2$ tsp salt then press half the mixture into each prepared cake tin and bake in a very low oven, approximately Gas Mark 1 (140ºC) for 30–40 minutes until firm to the touch.
4. Soften the Quark or soft cream cheese in a bowl with another 2 tsp of vanilla essence and use half to sandwich the two cakes together. Spread the other half over the top of the cake.
5. Use a rolling pin or similar to crush the Dime bars between a large folded sheet of greaseproof paper and put the broken bars in a Pyrex bowl over a saucepan of hot water until the chocolate has melted completely.
6. Spread the melted Dime bar mixture over the top of the cake and refrigerate.

TUTTI-FRUTTI ICE CREAM

This is easily the best ice cream I've ever made (not having an ice cream maker) and once again you don't have to be too precise with the quantities; as long as the tins and cartons are roughly the same size the recipe should work.

I tried replacing the fruit with Jelly Tots once but the freezing process made the sweets too hard and gooey and potentially hazardous to kids' teeth, although I don't see why you couldn't make a chocolate chip version, or maybe use fresh apricots or raspberries if you wanted to.

The quantities given here are perfect for a standard 2 lb (1 kg) loaf tin.

1 tin of condensed milk
$^1/_2$ standard tin of coconut milk
1 carton of ready-made custard (500 g)
1 large carton of double cream (284 ml)
2 tbsp vanilla essence
A handful each of dried apricots, glacé cherries and raisins

Method

1. Line a standard loaf tin or bowl with a double layer of cling film with plenty of overlap around the sides and chop the fruit into small pieces.
2. Beat the cream in a large bowl with an electric hand whisk until just standing up in soft peaks, but try not to over-beat so it goes all thick and holey.
3. Add the custard, condensed milk, coconut milk and vanilla essence and beat again on the lowest speed setting for another minute, or less, to combine everything together. (Don't worry if the mixture isn't completely smooth.)
4. Scatter the fruit into the bowl so it doesn't stick together in big lumps, stir well, then scoop the mixture into the lined loaf tin or bowl.
5. Cover the ice cream with another double layer of cling film and freeze for 6–8 hours. Once the ice cream has been frozen overnight, allow it to stand at room temperature for a couple of minutes before serving, as you would with most other ice creams.
6. Serve in bowls or cornet wafers.

MAGIC CHOCOLATE PUDDING

This must be one of the all-time perfect puddings. The mixture separates during cooking to produce a soft, light sponge with a thick chocolate sauce underneath, and it's easy enough for older kids to make by themselves. (My 15-year-old daughter Eleanor and her friend Jessie made it at our house recently when I was out.)

The quantities below make a very large pudding, which should be enough for at least eight people, so make half this amount if you want a medium-sized pudding or six small individual puddings.

10 oz (275 g) plain flour
4 tsp baking powder
¹/₂ tsp salt
4 oz (100 g) caster sugar
4 tbsp cocoa powder
4 oz (100 g) butter or margarine
2 eggs
2 tsp vanilla essence
1 mug of milk

For the topping
3 tbsp soft brown sugar
3 tbsp cocoa powder
1¹/₂ mugs of boiling water

Method
1. Lightly butter a large soufflé dish (or several small ones) and preheat the oven to Gas Mark 4 (180°C).
2. Sift the flour, baking powder, cocoa powder, sugar and salt into a very large mixing bowl and make a well in the centre.

3. Melt the butter and add to the dry ingredients with the milk, eggs and vanilla essence then mix everything together thoroughly with a large metal spoon.
4. Pour the mixture into the prepared dishes then sprinkle the entire surface of the pudding(s) with the soft brown sugar and cocoa powder.
5. Now carefully pour the boiling water over the pudding(s) as evenly as you can and bake in the oven for 30–40 minutes, until the sponge is firm and springy to the touch.
6. Serve with cream.

BAKEWELL TART

Use raspberry jam instead of apricot and make a thin layer of glacé icing for the top rather than dusting with icing sugar if you prefer – and if you use a ready-made pastry case you can skip the whole of the first method altogether.

For the pastry
1 oz (25 g) butter or margarine
1 oz (25 g) lard or Cookeen
4 oz (100 g) plain flour
4 tbsp milk (or water, or some of each)
1 tbsp sugar

Method
1. Preheat the oven to Gas Mark 5 (190ºC) and lightly grease a flan tin or pie dish approximately ½ in (1.25 cm) deep and 8 in (20 cm) across.
2. Sift the flour into a large mixing bowl, add the fat in small pieces and rub in until the mixture resembles medium-fine

breadcrumbs, then stir in the sugar.

3. Make a well in the centre of the flour, pour in the milk and/or water and mix together to make a firm, smooth dough.

4. Turn the dough out onto a floured surface, knead for a couple of minutes then roll out the pastry to fit the flan tin and trim away the excess.

5. Prick the bottom of the flan with a fork a few times and bake blind for about 15 minutes until the pastry looks slightly crisp but not quite golden. (To bake blind: cover the bottom of the flan case with a piece of greaseproof paper and weigh down with dried beans, rice or lentils.)

6. Remove the beans and greaseproof paper and return the flan case to the oven for another 5 minutes to crisp up the pastry.

For the filling

3 oz (75 g) butter or margarine
3 oz (75 g) sugar
2 eggs, separated
3 oz (75 g) self-raising flour
4 tbsp ground almonds
Milk
Apricot jam

Method

1. Put butter and sugar in a large mixing bowl and beat together with an electric whisk until pale and fluffy.

2. Add the egg yolk all at once, beating continuously to stop the mixture curdling.

3. Stir in the flour and ground almonds with a metal spoon and add a splash of milk to get the mixture to a soft, dropping consistency.

4. Whisk the egg whites till stiff in a separate, much smaller bowl

– don't bother to clean the blades first – then fold into the rest of the mixture.

5. Spread the bottom of the flan case with a thick layer of jam then fill to the top with the cake mixture.

6. Bake in the oven at Gas Mark 5 (190ºC) for about 25 minutes. Allow to cool and dust with icing sugar.

BAKED ALASKA

Baked Alaska must have been even easier to put together when you could still buy ice cream in solid blocks – or maybe you still can, I never see it like that now though – but even if you decide to bake the sponge yourself and make a fresh fruit purée instead of opening a tin, this impressive little pudding is a nice easy one for absolute beginners to make, or indeed anyone who wants something sweet after dinner in a lot less time than it takes to open the box and leave a supermarket dessert to defrost.

Anyway, you can elaborate on the cheat's version of Baked Alaska and make as many improvements as you like. This is just the recipe in its most basic form.

1 large ready-made sponge flan case
Vanilla ice cream
1 tin of mixed berries or summer fruits
4 egg whites
3 tbsp caster sugar

Method

1. Stand the sponge flan case on a cold oven tray and preheat the oven to Gas Mark 6 (200°C).
2. Take the ice cream straight from the freezer without allowing it to sit in the fridge or stand at room temperature first, and put as many scoops into the flan case as it takes to make a gently rounded dome on top of the sponge without overdoing it. (As a very rough guide I'd say the ice cream should be no more than about 3 ½ in (9 cm) high in the middle – but that's only guessing. Just do what looks right to you.)
3. Pile the tinned fruit (without the juice) around the ice cream, neatly filling in any gaps to make the pudding as smooth and compact as possible.
4. Whisk the egg whites and about half the quantity of caster sugar with an electric hand whisk until the meringue stands up in peaks and you can turn the bowl upside down without the contents sliding out then fold in the remainder of the sugar.
5. Smooth the meringue all over the top of the fruit and ice cream in an even layer, making sure it meets the sponge around the edge, then fluff the meringue up a bit with a fork or blunt knife – or do whatever you think makes the pudding look good. (You could use a star-shaped nozzle and a large piping bag to create a more elaborate pattern with the meringue if you can be bothered. I never can.)
6. Put the pudding at the bottom of the oven on Gas Mark 6 (200°C) for about 10 minutes, until the meringue is dried out and golden in places.

TRIFLE

Let's face it, trifle has a bit of a downmarket image these days, probably because it's so readily available in packets and plastic pots, most of which, embarrassingly, are actually quite addictive and appealing even in their most synthetic supermarket form. Anyway, here's a proper old-fashioned type of trifle that's well worth making from time to time, and which you don't need to feel ashamed of.

(If you want the cake to be home-made, make an all-in-one Victoria sponge from a mixture of 4 oz (100 g) each of self-raising flour, sugar and margarine with 2 eggs.)

1 large Madeira cake
1 tin of apricots
1 packet of orange jelly
1 very large glass of sherry (or more)
1 egg
2 egg yolks
1 tbsp caster sugar
1 tbsp cornflour
³⁄₄ pint (450 ml) milk
1 carton of double or whipping cream
Glacé cherries
Flaked almonds

Method
1. Break up the sponge cake and arrange in the bottom of a large cut-glass serving bowl then pour the sherry over the sponge and leave to soak.
2. Drain the tin of apricots, covering the sponge with the fruit, then make up the jelly according to the instructions on the packet, using the juice from the tin of apricots instead of cold water.

3. While the jelly is cooling, make the custard by mixing the egg, egg yolks and sugar together in a bowl. In a cup, blend the cornflour with a few tablespoons of milk from the ³/₄ pint (450 ml) then add that to the eggs and sugar and mix to a paste.

4. Meanwhile, warm the rest of the milk in a large saucepan until it comes up to the boil then pour the hot milk onto the paste, stirring constantly.

5. Pour the custard back into the pan and, still stirring all the time, cook over a low heat for a couple of minutes until the custard has definitely turned, meaning it's thick and creamy enough to coat the back of a spoon.

6. Pour the custard into the bowl again and leave to cool, either covered with a layer of cling film or sprinkled with a couple of teaspoons of sugar and a little cold milk to prevent a skin forming. (Alternatively, put the custard in a blender or food processor and turn it onto the slowest setting for a minute at a time until the custard is almost cold.)

7. While the custard is cooling, pour the cold jelly over the fruit and sponge and refrigerate.

8. Pour the cold custard over the trifle and chill for a few hours before topping with the whipped cream. Decorate with halved glacé cherries and flaked almonds.

HOT FUDGE SUNDAES

This simple hot fudge sauce will keep for about a week in the fridge, which is just as well since a little of it goes a long way, so don't get carried away and pour too much over the fruit and ice cream, you really don't need it.

Alternatively, have this sauce with sliced bananas and chopped almonds or hazelnuts.

For the sauce
1 tin of condensed milk
4 oz (100 g) plain chocolate
2–3 tbsp maple or golden syrup (or a mixture of each)

1 tin of maraschino cherries
Vanilla and/or chocolate ice cream
Flaked or crushed almonds

Method
1. Put the condensed milk in a heatproof bowl with the broken up chocolate over a saucepan of previously boiled water and leave for about 15 minutes until the chocolate has melted completely.
2. Add the syrup to the sauce and stir well.
3. Layer a scoop of each flavour of ice cream into sundae glasses or bowls with the cherries; pour a couple of tablespoons of hot fudge sauce over each one and top with a small handful of nuts.

QUICK QUEEN OF PUDDINGS

Like Steamed Syrup Sponge and Nursery Pudding this is another very old classic English dessert that has several variations. This is the easiest – surprise, surprise – and if you want to make it in advance, let the pudding cool down once the custard has been baked at step 6; keep it in the fridge then let it stand at room temperature for about half an hour before you top with the meringue and finish it off in the oven.

$^1/_2$ lb (225 g) sponge cake

1 pint (600 ml) milk

2 dessertspoons of sugar

3–4 tablespoons of raspberry or apricot jam, or lemon curd

2 eggs, separated

2 tsp vanilla extract

Butter

Method

1. Bring the milk to the boil in a saucepan over a medium heat.
2. Meanwhile separate the eggs and keep the whites covered in the fridge for later. Beat the egg yolks together with the vanilla extract in another cup or small bowl, and in a large bowl break the sponge cake up into crumbs with your hands.
3. Butter a medium-sized oven dish all over and spread a fairly thick layer of jam or lemon curd across the bottom.
4. As soon as the milk is hot enough – it doesn't have to come right up to the boil, but there should be bubbles, or a thin, crinkly skin forming on the surface – pour it into the large bowl with the cake crumbs and mix well.
5. Stand the bowl by an open window to cool for about 5 minutes; meanwhile preheat the oven to Gas Mark 4 (180ºC).
6. As soon as the milk and sponge mixture has cooled down a bit stir in the egg yolks and vanilla extract then pour the custard into the oven dish and bake for 20–25 minutes until just set. (When you take the custard out, turn the oven down to its lowest setting.)
7. Allow the custard to cool for a few minutes.
8. Whisk the egg whites and half the sugar with an electric hand whisk until the meringue is standing up in stiff peaks. Add the rest of the sugar and gently fold it in with a metal spoon.
9. Spoon the meringue over the top of the custard, making sure

the surface is covered; fluff the meringue up with a blunt knife or make swirls with a fork to make it look good. (Or pipe the meringue on with a star-shaped nozzle.)

10. Bake the pudding in a *very* cool oven for about 45 minutes to one hour until the meringue is crisp, dried out and very slightly golden in places, and the custard has warmed through. Serve with evaporated milk or single cream.

NURSERY PUDDING

Nursery puddings are generally made from a concoction of fruit, stale sponge or soft white bread and some kind of custard or cream. There are dozens of variations to be found in really old cookery books; this recipe is nursery pudding in its simplest form, but it could also be made with fresh fruit and a proper home-made custard sauce. I've taken the easy route here and used a tin of mixed summer fruits in natural juice and blancmange made from the packet. (The instructions for making blancmange are on the box but I've included them here too.)

Stewed apples in sweet, spicy syrup with vanilla blancmange or custard would be another good combination, as would sliced bananas sprinkled with brown sugar and nutmeg, with chocolate blancmange or custard.

The amount of sponge cake used here – and this also applies to the Quick Queen of Puddings recipe – is the equivalent of a sponge made with 2 oz (50 g) each of butter, sugar and flour with one egg; i.e. one half of a Victoria Sandwich, or an average shop-bought sponge cake.

$^{1}/_{2}$ lb (225 g) of sponge cake
1 tin of mixed summer fruits in natural juice

1 sachet of strawberry blancmange
3 dessertspoonfuls of sugar
1 pint (600 ml) milk

Method
1. Empty the contents of one sachet of pink blancmange into a large bowl with 2 spoonfuls of sugar and mix to a paste with a very little milk from 1 pint (600 ml).
2. Bring the rest of the milk slowly to the boil until bubbles are forming on the surface then pour a little of the warm milk into the bowl with the blancmange paste and keep stirring as you pour the rest of the milk into the bowl.
3. Pour the blancmange back into the pan and bring to the boil over a low heat, stirring all the time, and simmer for about one minute until the blancmange is thick, smooth and creamy, just like custard.
4. Pour the blancmange back into the bowl and leave to cool by an open window for about 10 minutes, whisking with a fork from time to time. (The blancmange doesn't have to cool completely; lukewarm is fine.)
5. Meanwhile, cut the sponge cake into neat $1/4$ inch (5 mm) slices and cover the bottom of a medium-sized baking dish, a couple of inches (about 5 cm) deep, then spoon all the juice from the tin of fruit into the dish to soak the sponge.
6. Cover the sponge with the fruit then pour on the slightly cooled blancmange and sprinkle the last dessertspoonful of sugar evenly across the surface to stop a skin forming. Refrigerate for an hour or two until the blancmange is set.

BUTTERSCOTCH CRUNCH

Not long ago I read that Heston Blumenthal gave butterscotch Angel Delight the thumbs up (at least he said he quite liked it), which is a good enough reason to include it here. In fact, lots of people must like Angel Delight, secretly or otherwise, or it wouldn't still be going strong after all these years (see also Classics: Spam Fritters.) The only problem is it doesn't keep well so don't make it too far in advance.

Serve individually in small wine glasses or ramekins – allowing, say, one ginger biscuit per person – and if you're making it for more than six people, use two packets of Angel Delight and double up the quantities of everything else.

6 ginger biscuits
1 oz (25 g) butter
1 packet of butterscotch Angel Delight
1 small carton of double cream
Milk
Hazelnuts

Method

1. Crush the ginger biscuits into crumbs and mix with the melted butter in the usual way then put a spoonful into the bottom of each glass or ramekin, pressing down in an even layer to make the bases.

2. Empty the packet of Angel Delight into a bowl, pour the carton of cream into a measuring jug and top up with fresh milk to about ½ pint (300 ml) then make up the whip according to the instructions on the packet.

3. Break up a handful of hazelnuts and stir through the made-up Angel Delight; fill the glasses or ramekins with whip and decorate with whole hazelnuts.

FRUIT COBBLER

Vary the type and quantity of the fruits to suit yourself, but the colours in this are very appealing when you use the apricots and cranberries together, bearing in mind that the fruit's not completely covered by the pastry the way it would be with a regular pie or crumble.

I've only included the minimum amount of sugar here so you may want to add a bit more – or a couple of spoonfuls of golden syrup – for extra sweetness.

4 large Bramley apples (or 2 tins of apple chunks)
$1/4$ bag of mixed fruit or sultanas
$1/2$ bag of dried apricots
1 small packet of dried cranberries
1 tsp mixed spice
3 tbsp brown sugar
4 tbsp self-raising flour (plus extra for dusting)
2 tbsp natural yoghurt

Method
1. If using fresh apples, peel, slice and stew the fruit in a little water with a couple of tablespoons of sugar (apart from the 3 tbsp in the list of ingredients) until almost soft.
2. Mix the apples and remaining fruit together with approximately 2 tablespoons of sugar and 1 teaspoon of mixed spice in a large ovenproof dish, adding more or less of each

according to taste.

3. Sift the flour and the remaining tablespoon of sugar into a mixing bowl, make a well in the centre then add the yoghurt and stir with a spoon or a blunt knife until the mixture comes together to make a soft, sticky dough.

4. Form the dough into small, fairly flat scones with your hands and place at intervals across the top of the fruit.

5. Bake in a preheated oven, Gas Mark 4 (180ºC) for 20–25 minutes until the fruit is hot and the pastry is golden. Serve on its own or with cream or evaporated milk.

SIMPLE PINEAPPLE SORBET

1 fresh pineapple
$^1/_2$ pint (300 ml) water
4 tbsp sugar
or
2 tins of pineapple + juice or syrup
2 egg whites

Method

1. If using fresh pineapple, put the sugar and water in a small saucepan over a very low heat until all the sugar has dissolved then turn the heat up and boil for a couple of minutes to make a syrup.

2. Purée the pineapple – fresh or tinned – in a blender or food processor then mix the pulped fruit with the syrup (allow the syrup to cool down a bit if you've made fresh) and put it in the freezer in a large food bag for about 3 hours until mushy.

3. Whisk the egg whites until stiff then fold into the fruit and return to the freezer for at least a couple of hours, or overnight.

4. Put the sorbet in the fridge for about 15 minutes to soften slightly when you're ready to eat it and spoon out of the bag with an ice cream scoop to serve.

PIZZA

Just when you thought pizza's been done every which way already, here's another thing.

These pizzas are made with the pastry dough in the Super-Quick-No-Wait Pizza recipe in Chapter 2, 'Kids' Favourites' but I see no reason why sweet pizzas couldn't be made with regular yeast dough, and now we're used to the idea of everyday foods made with quirky ingredients – beetroot in chocolate cake is one – why wouldn't anyone be prepared to give blueberry and ricotta pizza a try?

It takes a genius to make snail porridge and bacon and egg ice cream appealing, but to Heston Blumenthal these pizzas would seem positively mundane, and when you think about it, in principle they're no different from any other kind of sweet pastry or cheesecake really. So give them a go – they're unbelievably quick and easy to make – and then decide. (The five flavours here have all been tried, tested and approved, but there must be more.)

And finally, if you find this dough doesn't crisp up enough in the cooking time – and this applies when you're making it with savoury toppings as well – put the pizza bases in the oven for 5 – 10 minutes first to give them a head start.

This amount of dough is enough for two 9 in (23 cm) pizzas.

8 rounded tbsp of self-raising flour (8 oz/200 g)
2 tsp baking powder

1 tbsp sugar
2 oz (50 g) butter or margarine
2 eggs
4 tbsp milk

Method
1. Sift the flour, baking powder and sugar into a large mixing bowl, stir well then add the melted butter, milk and beaten egg.
2. Mix everything together with your hand and pinch the dough together into a soft ball.
3. Turn the dough out onto a floured surface and knead very gently for a minute or just long enough to make it smooth and ready to roll.
4. Divide the dough in two, roll out each piece into a rough circle and either press into two well-greased 9 in (23 cm) cake tins or put the bases on oiled baking trays. Fold the rough edges inwards and press into shape to make them neater.
5. Add the topping and bake in the oven on Gas Mark 4–5 (180–190ºC) for 20–25 minutes.

Apricot & Marshmallow

Lemon curd or apricot jam
1 tin of apricots
Mini white marshmallows

Method
1. Spread the pizza base with lemon curd or apricot jam.
2. Drain the tin of apricots, chop or slice the fruit and cover the surface of the pizza, filling in the gaps with the marshmallows.

3. Bake the pizza on Gas Mark 4 (180ºC) for about 20 minutes until the marshmallows are puffing up and turning slightly brown.

Chocolate Orange & Ginger

Apricot jam
1 tin of mandarin segments
1–2 oz (25–50 g) chocolate (dark or milk)
$^1/_2$ tsp ginger (or use fresh)

Method
1. Spread the pizza base with apricot jam.
2. Drain the tin of mandarin segments and cover the surface of the pizza with the fruit.
3. Sprinkle or grate the ginger evenly over the fruit according to taste and roughly grate the chocolate on top.
4. Bake for about 20 minutes, Gas Mark 4 (180ºC).

Apple, Sultana & Mozzarella

Redcurrant jelly
1 tin of apples
Sultanas
1 tsp mixed spice
Mozzarella cheese

Method
1. Spread the pizza base with redcurrant jelly.
2. Drain the tin of apples and mash the fruit up a bit with a fork. Wash the sultanas in plenty of warm water and dry with an old clean tea towel or kitchen roll.
3. Cover the surface of the pizza with the mashed up apple and sultanas and sprinkle with the mixed spice.
4. Top with grated mozzarella and bake the pizza at Gas Mark 5 (190ºC) for about 20 minutes, or until the cheese is brown and bubbling.

Blueberry & Ricotta

Redcurrant or cranberry jelly or raspberry jam
Blueberries
Ricotta cheese (or Quark)
1 tsp brown sugar
1 tsp cinnamon

Method
1. Spread the pizza base with jelly or jam.
2. Wash the blueberries and dry thoroughly then cover the pizza with the fruit.
3. Sprinkle the fruit with the sugar and cinnamon then dot all over with small spoonfuls of the ricotta or Quark.
4. Bake in the oven, Gas Mark 5 (190ºC), for 20–25 minutes.

Pina Colada

Lemon or pineapple curd
1 small tin of pineapple
2–3 tbsp desiccated coconut
2 tbsp sherry
2 tsp brown sugar

Method
1. Beat the lemon or pineapple curd together with the sherry and spread over the pizza base.
2. Drain the tin of pineapple and cut the fruit into small pieces.
3. Cover the pizza with the fruit, sprinkle the sugar on top then finish with the coconut.
4. Bake in the oven, Gas Mark 4 (180°C), for 20–25 minutes.

"I want to put a stop to wasted food.
Maybe we should scale back on our
portions and spread it around. There is so
much hunger in the world that I resent
being served more than I can eat."

Jessica Harris

6
A lot on your plate

*If you're really clever you should be able to come up with a menu plan
every week that not only saves time and a couple of trips to the
supermarket, but also carves a big chunk off your grocery bill.
Even if you're not really clever and just throw a handful of recipes
together according to what you fancy at the time, you should still find
you spend a lot less money than you would have done if you'd gone to
the supermarket without a plan, or at least a shopping list and a
rough idea of what you're going to cook every night.
There's enough food on these shopping lists to feed a family
of four to six people – depending on age, size and appetite – from
Monday to Friday.*

MENUS

Week One
Bean & Frankfurter Ragout *(Chapter 2: Classics, page 36)*
Falafel *(Chapter 2: Cool Dinners, page 104)*
Beef Teriyaki *(Chapter 2: Credit Crunch Cuisine, page 115)*
Pasta & Pesto *(Chapter 2: Credit Crunch Cuisine, page 131)*
Sweet & Sour Pork *(Chapter 2: Classics, page 32)*

Week Two
Baked Potato Fishcakes *(Chapter 3: Potatoes, page 195)*
Coronation Chicken *(Chapter 2: Cool Dinners, page 98)*
Roasted Vegetables with Red Onion & Roquefort *(Chapter 2:*

Credit Crunch Cuisine, page 120)
Creamy Pasta Bake *(Chapter 2: Classics, page 39)*
Lamb Keema *(Chapter 2: Curry, page 80)*

Week Three
Southern Fried Chicken *(Chapter 2: Kids' Favourites, page 143)*
Scotch Eggs *(Chapter 2: Cool Dinners, page 100)*
Squash & Salmon Fishcakes *(Chapter 4: Mains, page 211)*
Filo Pastry Pie *(Chapter 2: Credit Crunch Cuisine, page 121)*
Sticky Ribs *(Chapter 2: Kids' Favourites, page 145)*

Week Four
Baked Fish in Horseradish Sauce *(Chapter 4: Mains, page 233)*
Asparagus Quiche *(Chapter 2: Cool Dinners, page 95)*
Super-Quick-No-Wait-Pizza *(Chapter 2: Kids' Favourites, page 158)*
Potato Croquettes *(Chapter 3: Potatoes, page 188)*
Sausage & Potato Omelette *(Chapter 3: Leftovers, page 172)*

Week Five
Chicken Chasseur *(Chapter 2: Classics, page 13)*
Quick Curried Prawns *(Chapter 2: Curry, page 87)*
Sausages in Onion Gravy with Root Vegetable Crush *(Chapter 2: Comfort Food, page 57)*
Chips & Curry Sauce *(Chapter 2: Comfort Food, pages 43, 45)*
Sausage Chilli *(Chapter 3: Leftovers, page 170)*

Week Six
Chicken & Rosemary Pot Roast *(Chapter 2: Comfort Food, page 75)*
Leftover Chicken Pie *(Chapter 3: Leftovers, page 165)*
Vegetarian Moussaka *(Chapter 3: Potatoes, page 190)*
Swedish Meatballs *(Chapter 2: Comfort Food, page 51)*
Macaroni Cheese *(Chapter 2: Comfort Food, page 52)*

WEEK ONE

Bean and Frankfurter Ragout
Falafel and salad
Beef Teriyaki and rice
Pasta and Pesto
Sweet & Sour Pork

Basics & Store Cupboard Ingredients
Flour: cornflour, plain
Fats: oil, olive oil, butter or margarine
Herbs: parsley
Spices: cayenne pepper, coriander, cumin, garlic salt, ginger, onion salt
Salt & pepper
Garlic
Garlic purée, tomato purée
Black treacle
Jam
Mustard
Sherry
Soy Sauce
Vinegar

The Shopping List
Pork fillets (6 +)
Quorn beef-style pieces (12 oz/300 g) x 2
Frankfurters (10) x 2
Grated Parmesan (4 oz/100 g)
Eggs x 6
Dried kidney beans (1 lb/500 g)
Dried chickpeas (1 lb/500 g)

Rice (2 lb/1 kg)
Pasta (1 lb/500 g)
Pine nuts (4 oz/100 g)
Cider (4 pints/2 litres)
Lettuce
Tomatoes (1$^1/_2$ lb/750 g)
Cucumber
Green beans
Red onions
1 red pepper
Mushrooms
1 packet (1$^1/_4$ oz/30 g) fresh basil

WEEK TWO

Baked Potato Fishcakes with Tomatoes & Sweetcorn
Coronation Chicken and rice
Roasted Vegetables with Red Onion & Roquefort
Creamy Pasta Bake
Lamb Keema & rice

Basics & Store Cupboard Ingredients
Flour
Fats: oil, olive oil, butter or margarine
Herbs: parsley, mint
Spices: coriander, cumin, curry powder, turmeric
Salt & pepper
Garlic
Lemon juice
Lime juice

Porridge oats
Sugar
Tomato purée

The Shopping List
Chicken fillets or pieces (1 lb/ 500 g)
Lamb mince (1 lb/500 g)
Chorizo sausage (4 oz/100 g)
Fresh white fish (x 2 large fillets)
Milk (1 litre/2 pints)
Natural yoghurt (1 lb/500 g)
Cheddar (½ lb/250 g)
Rice (2 lb/1kg)
Pasta (1 lb/500 g)
Couscous (1 lb/500 g)
Coconut milk (1 tin)
White wine (½ pint/250 ml)
Chopped tomatoes x 2
Garden peas (1 tin)
Sweetcorn
Apricots (1 tin)
Large baking potatoes
Butternut squash
Mixed peppers
Tomatoes
Carrots
Onions
Red onions
Mushrooms

WEEK THREE

Everything on the list this week can be served with potatoes and salad.

Southern Fried Chicken
Scotch Eggs
Squash & Salmon Fishcakes
Filo Pastry Pie
Sticky Ribs & Sausages

Basics & Store Cupboard Ingredients
Flour: plain, cornmeal (yellow maize)
Fats: oil, olive oil, butter or margarine
Herbs: basil, chives, thyme, marjoram
Spices: allspice, cayenne pepper, celery salt, chilli powder, coriander, cumin seeds, garlic salt, nutmeg, onion salt, paprika
Salt & pepper
Clear honey
Lemon juice
Mayonnaise
Mustard
Vinegar

The Shopping List
Chicken pieces on the bone x 2 packs (12)
Pork mince (1 lb/500 g)
Pork ribs
Sausages x 2 packets (6)
Fresh salmon fillets (2)
Eggs x 12
Milk (2 pints/1 litre)

Sage and Onion stuffing (7 oz/170 g)
Bread
Filo pastry
Red pesto
Tomato juice (2 pints/1 litre)
Butternut squash
New potatoes (5 lb/2.5 kg)
Lettuce x 2
Tomatoes
Cucumber x 2
Watercress
Radishes
Spinach
Courgettes x 3
Spring onions

WEEK FOUR

Baked Fish in Horseradish Sauce
Asparagus Quiche
Super-Quick-No-Wait-Pizza
Potato Croquettes
Sausage & Potato Omelette

Basics & Store Cupboard Ingredients
Flour: cornflour, plain, self-raising, baking powder
Fats: oil, olive oil, butter or margarine
Herbs: parsley
Spices: paprika
Salt & pepper
Garlic purée

Tomato purée
Horseradish
Lemon juice
Mustard

The Shopping List
Sausages x 2 packets (6)
Fresh white fish
Eggs x 12
Cheshire cheese (8 oz/250 g)
Cheddar (8 oz/250 g)
Feta (7–8 oz/200 g)
Mozzarella (8 oz/250 g)
Natural yoghurt (1 lb/500 g)
Single cream ($^1/_2$ pint/300 ml)
Bread
Quinoa (12 oz/300 g)
Broad beans
Potatoes (5 lb/2.5 kg)
Spring onions
Asparagus
Tomatoes
Green beans
Mushrooms
Mustard & cress

WEEK FIVE

Chicken Chasseur
Quick Curried Prawns
Sausages in Onion Gravy with Root Vegetable Crush
Chip Shop Curry Sauce
Sausage Chilli

Basics & Store Cupboard Ingredients

Flour: plain, gram
Fats: oil, olive oil, butter or margarine
Herbs: tarragon
Spices: allspice, chilli powder, cinnamon, cumin, cumin seeds, curry
  powder, ginger
Salt & pepper
Garlic purée
Tomato purée
Chicken stock
Gravy browning
Lemon juice
Sugar
Worcestershire sauce

The Shopping List

Chicken thighs x 2 packs (6+)
Sausages x 3 packets (6)
Frozen prawns x 1 large packet
Rice (2 lb/1 kg)
Red pesto
White wine ($1^1/4$ pints/750 ml)
Sultanas (1 lb/500 g)
Natural yoghurt (1 lb/500 g)

Chopped tomatoes
Potatoes (5 lb/2.5 kg)
Button mushrooms
Onions
Celery
Red and green peppers
Tomatoes
Cooking apples (2 lb/1kg)
Carrots
Turnip
Parsnips
Swede

WEEK SIX

Chicken & Rosemary Pot Roast
Leftover Chicken Pie
Vegetarian Moussaka
Swedish Meatballs
Macaroni Cheese

Basics & Store Cupboard Ingredients
Flour: cornflour, plain
Fats: oil, olive oil, butter or margarine
Herbs: Herbes de Provence, rosemary
Spices: cayenne pepper, garlic salt, nutmeg, onion salt
Salt & pepper
Tomato purée
Chicken or vegetable stock
Instant gravy granules
Gravy browning

Mustard
Sugar

The Shopping List
1 large whole chicken
Beef mince (1 lb/500 g)
Back bacon ($\frac{1}{2}$ lb (250 g)
Puff pastry (1 lb/500 g)
Eggs x 12
Milk (2 pints/1 litre)
Cheddar (8 oz/250 g)
Parmesan (4 oz/100 g)
Feta (7–8 oz/200 g)
Crème fraîche (1 lb/500 g)
Evaporated milk (7 fl oz/170 g)
White wine ($1\frac{1}{4}$ pints/750 ml)
Baked beans x 2 tins
Chopped tomatoes
Condensed soup
Sweetcorn
Redcurrant jelly
Macaroni (1 lb/500g)
Potatoes (5 lb/2.5 kg)
Aubergine
Courgettes
Red onions
Carrots
Celery
Onions
Broccoli
Spinach

MORE ABOUT BASICS

With good basics and store cupboard items, three key ingredients are often all you need to make several meals:

Minced beef or lamb
Potatoes
Onions

1. Shepherd's Pie
2. Swedish Meatballs
3. Meatball Curry
4. Lamb Keema
5. Pie & Mash & Liquor
6. Potato Croquettes

Also: Spaghetti Bolognese, Chilli con Carne, Rissoles

Minced pork
Sausages
Eggs

1. Raised Pork Pie
2. Scotch Eggs
3. Kebabs
4. Sausage & Egg Muffins
5. Chilli Dogs

Also: Sausage rolls, Sausage Omelette, Pork Meatballs

Pasta
Chopped tomatoes
Cheese

1. Cream of Tomato Soup
2. Macaroni Cheese
3. Hot Tomato Jelly
4. Pasta Bake
5. Pasta Soup

Also: Simple pasta sauce, pasta salads

Tuna
Potatoes
Sweetcorn

1. Baked Potato Fishcakes
2. Quick Baked Fishcakes
3. Fishcakes and chips

Also: Simple fish pie, tuna sandwiches

Basics and store cupboard ingredients can also be the foundation for a meal or a dish by themselves:

1. Falafel
2. Cheesy Corn Fritters
3. Cheese and Tomato Pizza
4. Curried Rice & Lentils
5. Home-Baked Beans
6. Barbecue Beans
7. Bean & Frankfurter Ragout

Also: Sweetloaf, Sweet Pastries, Profiterols, Steamed Syrup Sponge, Rice Pudding, Gipsy Tart, Bakewell Tart
Plus: Bread, pancakes, cakes and biscuits

"I never see any home cooking. All I get is fancy stuff."

HRH The Duke of Edinburgh

Index